MARKING TIME

MARKING TIME

*47 Reflections on Mark's Gospel for Lent,
Holy Week and Easter*

Nick Baines

SAINT ANDREW PRESS
Edinburgh

To
RONALD FORWARD

First published in 2005 by
SAINT ANDREW PRESS
121 George Street, Edinburgh EH2 4YN

Copyright © Nick Baines, 2005

ISBN 0 7152 0829 2

British Library Cataloguing in Publication Data
A catalogue record for this book is available from the British Library.

Typeset in Baskerville by Waverley Typesetters, Little Walsingham, Norfolk
Printed and bound by Bell & Bain Ltd, Glasgow

CONTENTS

ENDINGS AND BEGINNINGS

INTRODUCTION

A gospel such as Mark's is intended to be read in one go. It is not long and it is not difficult. But most people simply do not read any biblical book in a single sitting, and it is probably too optimistic to think that this is likely to change. That said, however, Mark has a fairly simple message to convey, and he will come at it from a series of perspectives.

Lent is a time for serious reflection on God, Christian discipleship and the nature of the good news of Jesus Christ. It is traditionally a season in which we take extra time to read, reflect and consider afresh the weighty matters of spiritual discipline. Furthermore, it is a period in which we strive to minimise distractions from what matters most essentially in Christian living, thinking and praying.

Lent, then, is a good time to read Mark's gospel and ask fundamental questions about God, Jesus and the people he invited to journey with him from a river to a cross and the embarrassment of an empty tomb in Jerusalem. Along the way, we meet people like us and we are challenged by the demands of God's call. But this is a journey we do not take in splendid individual isolation; we go in the company of others whom Jesus has also invited – regardless of whether we like, respect or agree with them.

This book is aimed at helping us to reflect on God, Jesus and Christian discipleship during Lent. It is further intended to help us get to know a gospel a little better and more coherently. It has, however, resulted in its final shape from a dilemma: do I take each passage consecutively, or do I take themes and then group passages accordingly? I have chosen the latter path, partly in order to allow for more effective reflection and group discussion of themes or characters, but always taking regard of the narrative context of any particular passage. One or two passages are not referred to separately (in their own section), but the issues they raise are covered by passages that are considered properly.

I am indebted to my wife, Linda, and my children – particularly Andrew, who still lives at home. Writing in the midst of a demanding life and full diary seems to take time from them, and it is they who deserve the blessing of God for the generosity of their spirit towards me.

This book is dedicated to the Revd Canon Ronald Forward, who was my Training Incumbent in the parishes of St Thomas, Kendal, and St Katherine, Crook, in Cumbria. I only shared the last three years of Ron's ministry there before he retired in 1990. His pastoral care, preaching and love of the Scriptures made a deep and lasting impression on me, shaping my ministry in ways he could not imagine. He and his wife, Mildred, are wonderful, and my debt to them is great.

Nick Baines
June 2005

testing of Jesus in the desert; but in one sense the vital bit of Mark's introduction comes in 1:15 when Jesus utters his first recorded words: 'The time is fulfilled, and the kingdom of God has come near; repent and believe in the good news'. This proclamation neatly envelops the introductory passage which establishes what Mark is doing by writing this little book: 'The beginning of the good news of Jesus Christ, the Son of God' (1:1).

This beginning matters for two reasons. Firstly, Mark's first words set out his store: Jesus of Nazareth is very good news … and the rest of this book will flesh out that bald statement. Secondly, Jesus' first words set out a manifesto that will be either vindicated or denied by the evidence of what follows. Jesus declares that now, in his person, the rule of God has come – God's time to act decisively is now upon the world, and the onus is on the world to respond. And what might that response look like? 'Repent and believe in the good news.'

Repentance does not have a good press these days. The Church, not famous for its unity and grace, freely uses the word to demand a change in the beliefs, values or behaviour of fellow Christians. Across the world, Christians often threaten each other that, unless things are done 'their way', relations will be broken. Repentance is always for those who are not like 'us' and who appear to commit the sins that 'we' do not. Repentance is a word thrown around too easily, often as a weapon by which to beat other believers. It is perhaps not so surprising that the people who most frequently call for repentance in others show little sign of the humility that leads to and emanates from their own repentance. After all, in another gospel, Jesus points out to the 'conservatives' that they study the Scriptures, believing that in them they will find life

– but, in fact, he is standing right there in front of them and they cannot see the obvious (John 5:39).

So, what is Jesus asking people to do, and why does he juxtapose 'good news' with something as miserable as 'repentance'? Doesn't he realise that asking people to change won't generally be heard as 'good' news? Anyway, what would ordinary Jews in Palestine make of this apparently arrogant interjection into their lives? These are the sort of questions that Mark expects the hearers or readers of his narrative to ask when being surprised by such bold language as that of his opening statement and Jesus' opening statement to the world.

To answer the questions, we must remember that the people are suffering under Roman occupation and there is no end in sight to the humiliation this represents. If God is God and these are his people, then why does he not vindicate the truth by booting the Romans out and establishing his people's true identity and destiny once and for all? He has done it before (the exodus from Egypt) and has promised to do it again – but still the 'exile' is not over. Messiahs have been popping up with great regularity, promising to lead the people in revolt, attempting to be the agent of God's deliverance of his people. But history has always told that God's hand will not be forced and God's passion will not be rushed. The time will come, but it will not be hastened by the urgency of people's demands, nor by the pain of their waiting.

So, the 'good news' of God's coming was bound to meet with a certain scepticism. How could this carpenter from Galilee possibly be the agent of deliverance? He and *whose* army? – as we might cynically pose the question today. So, when Jesus asks people to repent, he is not simply asking people to do something religious (like confess their sins in order to be free to carry on living their lives); rather, he is asking them to dare to *see* differently, to look at God, the world and themselves through a different lens, and therefore to glimpse the presence of God among them in a way they had never expected or conceived. This meant, first, allowing for the possibility that their deeply held and generally unquestioned religious, political and anthropological prejudices might be inadequate or misshapen; it meant having the courage to allow God to confound even those most sacred perceptions and convictions, opening them to be questioned, challenged or remoulded.

The time to repent is the time to let go of one way of seeing and thinking in order to embrace the risk of seeing and thinking differently and, therefore, living differently. Repentance – literally 'change of thinking' (*metanoia* in the Greek) – is what is required of the people of God first, and especially of those who believe themselves to be most godly, most orthodox, most right in their claims for God and his way of being with his people in the world.

It is not insignificant that we should begin Ash Wednesday, the introduction to the great season of waiting, reflecting, fasting and repenting, by stopping and hearing the powerful words of Jesus as he introduced his public ministry. But it might well be surprising that the call to repent, to see differently, will come to us as good news and not bad.

Lord God, Creator of all that is, you will not be hurried by the impatience of your people. As we hear afresh the call of Jesus to see differently, help us to recognise that the time has indeed come to recognise your presence in the world – in Jesus. Amen.

THURSDAY

MARK 1:14–15   BELIEVE THE GOOD NEWS

GIVEN the circumstances of first-century Jewish society, you would think that anyone bringing good news would be welcomed and embraced. You might expect that people would be glad to listen to anyone with an ounce of credibility who could bring a realistic hope of deliverance and peace. But even desperate people become sceptical of those purporting to bring good news after years and years (hundreds of them) of disappointment and disillusionment. They had been let down too often, and there was no sign yet that the day of deliverance was any closer than it had been in the past.

So, what would 'good news' have sounded like to the people of Jesus' time? Or, to put it a different way, what possible news might have sounded like good news to those people at that time? As I indicated yesterday, the only really good news would be that an army was being raised by God's agent in order to overthrow the Roman occupiers and restore sovereignty (both politically and theologically) to Israel. Nothing short of this sort of liberation would bring hope of a better life, of a restoration of dignity, of a realistic hope for future prosperity. This 'good news' would be associated with the coming again of God among the people, his presence restored and the blasphemy ended. Indeed, this 'time of fulfilment' would be obvious to all and unmistakable in the eyes of the watching world. How, then, would those who encountered Jesus proclaiming the 'good news of God' (1:14) have responded to the association of 'good news' with 'repentance'?

Mark knows what he is doing. Jesus, in his first utterances, subverts popular apprehensions of how the world is, how God is in that world and where God is to be seen and found in that world. The first thing people have to do if they are to hear the news of God's coming as 'good' is to think differently about who God is and how he might choose to act. Just suppose he came not as the general of a mighty army or the leader of a popular insurgency, but rather came as an ordinary man who invites people to change within their circumstances instead of only identifying God with acts that change those circumstances for the better? What, in other words, if God were to come among the people in the messiness of their real lives in a real historical context and bring the possibility of change within it rather than simply holding out the mere hope of a panacea from without? Would it not be good news indeed if God were to call for an end to the world's cycles of violence and powermongering and claim the vulnerability of the powerless 'Servant' as the greatest precondition for change and peace?

This might sound unremarkable to ears conditioned by 2,000 years of Christian language and teaching, but it was – and remains – deeply subversive of the way human beings usually (and uncritically) think of the world. The good news is primarily that God has come among us, as one of us, offering the sort of change of 'lens' (through which we see God, the world and ourselves) that will allow us to see as God sees, to lose our fear of our circumstances, to learn to wait for God's time, to be free from our imprisonment in the pit of worldly despair that only associates God's presence and activity with problem-free 'happiness' – or 'fantasy', as we should name it.

However, the interesting thing about Jesus' provocative proclamation is that he doesn't just expect people to hear differently and, hence, perceive his news as 'good'; he also expects those who hear to 'believe'. Unfortunately, the word 'believe' in English has now become anaemic. In popular western culture, 'belief' – especially religious belief – has become reduced to the status of mere opinion. It refers to a conviction or faith commitment that is either intellectual or emotional, but not usually susceptible to scrutiny or rational discussion. To believe in something or someone is simply a private matter for the individual and as such should not be aired in the public arena or at polite dinners. Furthermore, belief is frequently and unthinkingly associated with faith, which is, in turn, assumed to be the possession of people who cannot deal with brutal reality in the real world. This means, then, that we have to interpret the word 'believe' to a generation that might misunderstand what is meant by Jesus when he uses the word.

When Jesus invites people to believe the good news, he is not begging them to engage in a fantasy or pretend that things are better than they are. He is not telling them to suspend their intellectual faculties and ignore their observation of the world around them. He is not requiring them simply to appropriate an idea that might stimulate their imagination for a while, like a new theory about the Loch Ness Monster might do. No. Jesus is, in fact, asking far more than this: he is asking for a commitment of life – intellectual, spiritual, financial, social, physical, emotional – to the truth about God they have apprehended as 'good news'. In other words, if this news, this way of seeing and hearing differently is good and liberating, then it will cost you everything: your life and the commitment of that life to the truth of the news itself, the truth about God, his nature and his priorities.

Jesus is not a plaything, someone inoffensive who might just add the final polish to a satisfying life. Rather, he is the one who in himself brings subversively good news about God that some people will inevitably find to be very bad news about themselves. The world and its people will find in this man a challenge to their ways of seeing and hearing and thinking and living. He will call people to take seriously the character of God and to stop playing with their religion in such a way that its subject and object get lost somewhere in the system. He will call people – sometimes the 'wrong' people and always surprising people – to commit everything to what they only gradually glimpse of God and his ways, enfleshed in this Jesus. The invitation is almost reckless in its audacity. But Jesus will prove to be the most realistic man on the planet, and never a fantasist who leads people into a world of safe illusion within which they can hide from reality.

And he calls it 'good news' and invites us to respond.

Lord God, you created everything and us in your image. You call us to give you everything and live according to your image in us. Help us to commit ourselves and all we have to the good news that you are as you are in Jesus, that we can see everything through his eyes and be changed. Amen.

FRIDAY

MARK 1:1–11   WHOSE SIDE ARE YOU ON?

ANYONE who has supported a successful football club will understand what it means to 'prepare the way'. Standing among the excited crowds lining the streets to welcome the victorious team, displaying their trophies atop their open-topped bus as they wind their way to a civic reception, you know the time is coming when the police tell you to get off the road and onto the pavement. Then you hear the drone of the police motorcycles as they clear the way for the ensuing bus. First the motorbikes, then the bus.

Mark never saw a football match, but the experience of military and civic processions, preceded by heralds and way-clearers, was not unknown to him. But Mark is an impatient writer and wants to cram as much as possible into as few words as possible. He wants to evoke associations and conjure images that say a lot without wasting precious breath. Hence, he boldly states his purpose in writing this book ('The beginning of the good news of Jesus Christ, the Son of God', 1:1) before launching straight into more than half a millennium of history, association, hope and longing – all in the space of just a few verses. He quotes Isaiah, thus linking the prophetic promise of his people's Scriptures with John the Baptiser, who then indicates the association between the promise and its fulfilment in the person of Jesus of Nazareth.

Already, right at the outset of the gospel, Mark is inviting his hearers and readers to look for the evidence that will back up the audacious claims of verse 1. To put it simply, how are we to know that this Jesus *is* the Christ (the anointed one from God), the Son of God? Mark says that the answer is to be found by reading on and seeing whether or not the evidence of Jesus' life, words and actions reveals the character of God (which, you remember, might not be quite what you have been brought up to believe) and justifies the identity Mark attributes to him. John the Baptiser, says Mark, is the messenger who prepares the way for the enfleshed 'message', and the message speaks of the truth about God and his nature. And the message of John, baptising in the desert river those who perceive their need of forgiveness (never purely individualistic or private, but always both personal and national), is that the one who will make a reality of what this baptism promises is now among us and is one of us.

This is more powerful than it might at first seem to be. Mark has John playing the herald to the coming king, preparing the way so that the call by Jesus to a new way of thinking and seeing might possibly be heard. John uses language and rituals that open people's minds to the possibility that a new start might be possible, that the people's sins – identified with their continuing 'exile' – might soon be forgiven: that is, that the punishment represented by subjection might soon come to an end. It is not just private or personal regret about naughty things thought, said or done that drive people to be baptised by John in the Jordan; it is the recognition that the fate of the individual is caught up in the lot of the whole people, that they together need once again to be delivered by God.

Water washes clean, and John's baptism invites people to recognise their need to be washed in the first place. Here, we are back to our earlier observations about repentance: responding to the call to see differently presupposes an admission that one's current way of seeing might be either wrong or inadequate. In other words, only those people who had come to terms with their own sin or inadequacy were 'prepared' to be able to see differently when Jesus issued his call. John's job was to open people's minds and hearts so that the subversive call of Jesus might find at least some bit of soil in which to take root and from which to grow. John will provide a sign (water), the fulfilment or substance of which will be realised by Jesus. Promise will find fulfilment.

Yet, all of this points to something assumed by Mark. The call of Israel, from Abraham onwards, has been to be the people of God for the sake of the world, enfleshing God's ways and priorities, God's character and creative loving, in order that the whole world might be blessed. This calling, often compromised and perverted, is now being fulfilled in this man Jesus of Nazareth, and we will have to watch to see what this will mean in flesh-and-blood terms. John offers the long-held prophetic promise: Jesus will breathe the life (breath or spirit) of God himself and make real what John and all the great prophets could only point to.

But, if Jesus is the fulfilment of this promise, why did he volunteer to be baptised by John? The simple answer is that, in doing so, Jesus fully identified with this great prophetic tradition and took his place in it. You can only fulfil what you are committed to; you can only enflesh that to which you fully belong and with

11

which you fully identify. Jesus stands with his people, inheritor of the nation's history, victim of the people's predicament, fully identified with their plight – and thus able to embody their liberation from within.

The vindication of this tradition and Jesus' place within it comes with the epiphany of God's favour as Jesus emerges from the water. Appropriating the words of the psalmist, Jesus hears words of God's favour, and all seems bright and beautiful. Jesus is where he should be, and God is happy. Yet, again, Mark is teasing us with an apparent contradiction: God's favour on someone is recognised by how well things go for him, how wealthy she is, how comfortable life is for them. Here, however, we have God uttering words of utmost approval and blessing to one who will be ruthlessly opposed and eventually executed.

Do not read this gospel unless you are ready and willing to be surprised, even shocked. Do not read further if you are not prepared to risk your understanding of God himself and how Jesus of Nazareth is the icon of his nature.

Lord God, who in Jesus has come among us, fulfilling the longings of the prophets, thank you that you have fully identified with all your people in their messy humanity. Give us the courage to see afresh in the face of Mark's Jesus the subversive face of the Creator and Lover of all. Amen.

SATURDAY

MARK 1:12–13   WHAT SORT OF KINGDOM?
                WHAT SORT OF KING?

MARK tells us that, following his baptism by John in the River Jordan, Jesus was driven 'by the Spirit' out into the wilderness, where he was 'tempted by Satan' for forty days. How strange. Jesus emerges from the waters of baptism to hear the great words of affirmation from heaven; the next minute, that same 'Spirit' sends him into a hard place of discomfort and challenge. Surely Jesus needed some greater encouragement before embarking on what was to be a relatively short-lived public ministry. Would not a party have been of more use to him, building him up and demonstrating the truth of the affirmative words he had just heard from heaven?

Well, fortunately for us, God is not a sentimental deity whose main purpose in life is to keep his people happy all the time. God takes a long-term view of his people and of his Son. There will be plenty of time in the next couple of years for parties and celebrations as people embrace the presence of God's kingdom in the presence of Jesus among them. But now, right at the outset of Jesus' public ministry, there are more serious matters to attend to.

Mark doesn't give us any detail about the nature of the 'temptation' Jesus faced. Matthew and Luke tell a fuller story (chapter 4 of their respective gospels), but Mark just tells us it happened. Perhaps he assumed the details were more widely known and needed no further expansion. Or maybe the detail didn't seem pertinent to the particular task Mark had set himself in the writing of this gospel, and so he simply noted the event as part of the unfolding narrative and left the detail to the imagination. Or maybe the context of this remark and the brevity of its matter-of-fact description are all that is required to make the powerful point Mark wishes to represent.

Affirmation is fine, but it has to be earthed. Jesus has heard words of encouragement from heaven, but they themselves now beg the question of how 'Sonship' is to be exercised in real life and real choices. Pleasing God is not merely notional in nature, but essentially practical. The question that hovers over the narrative at this point is quite simply: if you are truly God's Son and the one anointed to call God's people to a new way of seeing and being, then what sort of kingdom is yours to be? What sort of 'Lord' will you be? Are you going to be like Israel, deviated from your calling and seduced by status, mistaking your vocation for privilege instead of responsible service, taking God for granted; or are you going to fulfil your calling whatever the cost? Will the people now see before their very eyes what God is truly like? Will those who are poor and marginalised find themselves surprised by God's welcome and lepers embraced by God's healing touch? Or will the powerful – especially the religious powerful – compromise you and neutralise the potency of your vision?

These are not trivial questions, and they are not the sort of questions that get answered in a single go. It is important, however, that the commencement of any serious mission is preceded by a serious wrestling with questions of true motivation and commitment. The search for a contemporary analogue does not take long. In his remarkable books *Stalingrad* and *Berlin: The Downfall 1945*, Antony Beevor has painfully and eloquently described the appalling human consequences of military generals (both Soviet and German) who lose sight of their strategic goal and use people as slaughter-fodder to advance their personal ambitions and play out their petty rivalries. Even though this motivation will be tested again and again, it is important to do some honest soul-searching right at the outset of any project – because the lives of others depend on it.

Of course, this episode is also intended to evoke echoes of Israel's own experience in its seminal liberation from captivity in Egypt. The glory days of the patriarchs had declined into servile exile in a foreign land, and the people could not save themselves. The Passover and exodus were costly events and depended on the initiative of God himself where human endeavour was hopeless. Jewish identity is rooted in this conviction, that God himself liberated his people and what he has done once he will do again. And the sequence was the same then as it is for Jesus now: the singular affirmation of the exodus was followed by a forty-year sojourn in the wilderness while one generation died out and the moaners and whingers learned that they still hadn't learned the lesson of their original calling.

So, Jesus is led into the desert 'by the Spirit' and not by his waywardness or sin. He is led into this time and place of testing not in spite of his faithfulness to God's call, but because of it. His mettle was to be tested and his resolve stretched. Satan would push him to the limit while his physical resources were low and his commitment vulnerable. He would face similar testings again in the next three or so years, but the onslaught here will prove what sort of 'Son' he might prove to be. From Matthew and Luke's expansions of this episode, we know that the temptations put to Jesus are those faced by all God's people: will you put material things above God's call? Will you run away from suffering and take the short-cut to glory? Will you take God and his favour for granted? Or will you fulfil the unfulfilled vocation of Israel – to lay down your life for your people, thus also demonstrating to a watching world what God is like and how far his love and mercy extend?

There are those today who see Jesus as a sort of Superman who probably spent these wilderness days doing press-ups in the sand, building up for the day of glory when he would surprise the world with his macho spirituality. Of course, this is rubbish and nonsense. Jesus faces his demons, the points of real vulnerability for him as a real human being who fully identifies with the rest of us: pride, hubris, fear and passion. The brevity of Mark's record should not be regarded as a diminution of its importance. The fact and context of its record should, indeed, cause us (as the Body of Christ – those called now to embody the same calling fulfilled by Jesus) to face the same questions with the same vulnerable honesty as did Jesus in his desert, noting that affirmation brings with it the threat of seduction and leads frequently to a Spirit-led sojourn in a dry place where God cannot be taken for granted and where the hard questions can no longer be avoided.

Lord God, whose Spirit both affirms us and refuses to coddle us, give us the grace to stay in the desert place when we are led there by you. Grant us the courage not to run away, but to await the time of our deliverance once the testing is done. Amen.

PERSONAL REFLECTION

In what way is Jesus 'good news' to me?

What does it mean for me to (a) 'repent' and (b) 'believe' that the kingdom of God is near?

GROUP DISCUSSION

1. What might it mean for us today, in our particular culture and church, to repent? How would people outside the Christian community recognise such repentance from and among Christians?

2. What might the following look like when seen through the eyes of Jesus:
    (a) God
    (b) history
    (c) religious people
    (d) us?

3. Are we willing to subject our deeply held convictions about God, Jesus and the world to scrutiny as we read this gospel? Or are we prepared only to hear and accept what conforms to our already-formed views?

CALLINGS

SUNDAY (LENT 1)

MARK 1:14–20   THE DISCIPLES

MARK is in a bit of a hurry. He does not want to delay too long before getting onto what he sees as the real business of Jesus, his words and actions. Having moved swiftly through Jesus' baptism and testing in the desert, he makes a passing remark about John the Baptiser's fate which serves to locate the events which are to follow.

Jesus is in Galilee, his home area. This is where he has grown up and worked and is the place where he is known. We will hear later how his family and friends are coping with the consequences of his new-found mission in life. But, for now, Mark moves us on. Time has clearly passed since Jesus met John the Baptiser in the desert, and now John has been arrested and imprisoned. Mark assumes his hearers and readers know the details and doesn't say more about it. But, brief though the reference is, it indicates the mood of the times. John is a disturber and has popular influence; the authorities are edgy about anyone who threatens to disturb the status quo. But, as John is silenced by removal from the scene, Jesus emerges onto the set with his bold proclamation. John has pointed towards the time to come; Jesus says that time has now come.

Jesus comes proclaiming 'the good news of God' and invites people to see differently and, therefore, to live differently – driven by the good news that God is once again visibly and actively among his people. But, of course, as hearers and readers of his text, we will ask: well, how did people respond, and what did this response look like in real human terms? So Mark tells us. And the story now gets going in earnest, the ground already set and assumed, the questions now evoked, and the curiosity of the audience awoken.

So, Jesus wanders along the beach watching people at work. He approaches Simon and Andrew and interrupts their labour with an extremely odd proposal: 'Follow me and I will make you fish for people'. Had I been in that boat in the middle of a working day, I don't think I'd have responded kindly. We must assume, however, that there was more to the conversation than this simple statement. Working men in a rural area do not simply leave their livelihood (especially when it is a family business) and wander off up the road with some stranger who has just appeared and said something bizarre to them.

But maybe this is Mark's point. Something in what Jesus said gave the two brothers a glimpse of a new way of seeing, and this was enough to tease their imagination and tickle their curiosity (or nosiness?). They left their nets and went with him. Further along the beach, they come across another two brothers, James and John, and a similar exchange takes place. They, too, leave their work and accompany Jesus, Simon and Andrew. Isn't that nice? Jesus isn't lonely any more and has some friends with whom to share his time and thoughts.

Or is there more to these two encounters than immediately meets the eye? Is Mark being suggestive once again instead of being expansive?

Whatever was said between Jesus and the two sets of brothers, and whatever they might or might not have understood Jesus to be about, we know that they responded to his call and went with him. But this meant that they had to leave some things behind them. A feature of Mark's understanding of what it meant for people to respond to Jesus' call to see differently and live differently is that it always involved leaving some things behind. In other words, there is always a cost to discipleship, always a change in circumstances. Those who choose to follow Jesus must do so without any illusion about the consequences: 'repentance' means loss of those things that belong to an old way of seeing and living. There has to be a leaving and a departure if the person is to move to a different place.

In one sense, this can be seen throughout the Scriptures. Abraham and Sarah had to leave Ur of the Chaldees in order to follow God's call. The blessing of all nations through him (Genesis 12:1–4) can only be realised if Abraham leaves and goes on a journey. Moses had to leave Egypt and then, later, the home and place of refuge and security, in order to follow God's call. He also had to leave behind his reluctance, lack of self-confidence and fear of failure. King David had to leave behind his glorious reputation for slaying giants and face up to his sexual failings and hypocrisy. And so it goes on, the whole of the Bible telling stories of people who, however feebly and falteringly, followed God's call by leaving behind either places, things, securities or people.

Now, if this seems harsh, look at it this way. Jesus is not asking of them what he has not already done himself. Furthermore, it is unrealistic anyway to think that it is ever possible to go on a journey from one place to another taking everything with you. It can't be

21

done. But Jesus makes the point clear that anyone who chooses to go with him for a walk up the beach must leave something behind in order to go. What's more, Simon, Andrew, James and John have no idea what lies in store for them, where the journey will take them or how their lives ultimately will change. And Jesus doesn't tell them.

Those who hear the call of Jesus and choose to follow him must suffer no illusions: they must take full personal responsibility for the choice they make and the consequences that choice will bring; they must recognise that some things must be left behind in order for the journey to begin; they will not have any claim to foreknowledge of what might lie in store for them in the future; they must go with the humility of inadequacy and ignorance. In fact, all they will have to rely on is the knowledge that Jesus himself has called them to see differently, to be brave enough and curious enough to want to explore what this might mean, and to be reckless enough to trust that the relationship with Jesus is enough to make the rest of it seem less important or vital.

Happiness is never once offered or guaranteed. All that is promised is a journey with Jesus into the unknown. Discipleship still starts here – even 2,000 years later and in a very different place and culture.

Lord God, we hear the voice of Jesus calling us to walk with him on a journey into unknown territory and unforeseeable experiences. Strengthen us for the cost and help us to walk with humility and curiosity as followers of him in the company of other fellow-travellers whom we have not necessarily chosen. Amen.

MONDAY (LENT 1)

Mark 1:18–20   Zebedee

ZEBEDEE is not a common name. In fact, there is a whole generation of middle-aged people in Great Britain who will respond to the mere mention of the name by whistling the theme tune to *The Magic Roundabout* and ending it with that great catchphrase: 'Time for bed, said Zebedee'. Very few people would immediately recall the father of James and John, the disciples of Jesus.

I have a soft spot for Zebedee for a whole host of reasons. Firstly, we know nothing about him other than that he was the father of these two sons. Secondly, he got the rough end of the deal when the two boys went walkabout with Jesus, leaving their work and their employer in the lurch. Thirdly, no preachers ever seem to talk about Zebedee except when reading the passage from the gospel, almost as if he has nothing to say to us. We might usefully dwell on these points briefly.

There is something about anonymity that is attractive – especially in a world where celebrity is lauded and every nobody in the world craves their fifteen minutes of fame, even if it comes by way of excruciating humiliation on a TV screen. We now live in a culture where nothing is regarded as private (except religious beliefs, of course) and everything is potentially exposed to the media spotlight – a world in which everybody claims a right to have a valid opinion about people they have never met and matters of which they are generally ignorant. Or that is how it can appear, at least, to watchers of television and readers of newspapers and magazines. However, the truth is that most human beings live ordinary and unremarkable lives, going about their business until they go to their graves. And they are spoken of in the Bible, because people like Zebedee are named and then ignored.

Zebedee was a father who apparently ran a family fishing business on the local sea. The sons (and maybe James and John weren't the only ones – we don't know) had serious responsibilities in both family and community, and it might never have occurred to them or their family and friends that life would change very much … ever. Zebedee might rationally and unquestioningly have assumed that his sons would work with him, eventually take over the business, then look after him and his family in his old age. For his sons simply to leave their work and responsibilities would have been unthinkable, even if Zebedee had hired workers with him. But the day came when they did. So, what is going on here?

James and John could probably not have simply left without at least conferring with their father. It might be reading too much into the text here, but this does suggest that Zebedee had some idea of what they were intending to do. Whatever the reality of the episode, it is interesting that the response by James and John to the call to follow Jesus also cost their father. Jesus does not appear to have invited him along too, but he pays a price for his sons' discipleship. They go, he stays; they have an adventure, he pays. So, where is the justice in that, and what might this say about the cost of following Jesus?

Maybe Zebedee's response to Jesus was not to go with Jesus, but rather to allow his sons to go while he picked up the slack which they left in their wake. Following Jesus was costly, but not primarily for James and John; it was their father who paid the price of their discipleship. Isn't this the unspoken flipside of real discipleship: that the discipleship and service of some people is only possible because of the cost to someone else – whose commitment and value is not highlighted or applauded as a model by preachers? This makes me (who, as a bishop in the Church of England, can only serve as I do because other people pay me a stipend and pension and provide me and my family with a house) wonder whether we have done justice to discipleship by only remarking on those who get the 'glory'. Most people follow Jesus in unremarkable ways through the everyday routines of life and loving. Nobody writes their biography or enshrines their heroism in stained glass as a teaching aid for young people. James and John have sermons preached about them and their discipleship while the response of their father to Jesus (equally important) goes unnoticed.

Following Jesus is not a simple matter, and yet our understanding of it can often be simplistic. Not everyone is called to be a James or a John. Not everybody is called to leave home and work and follow Jesus in a particular way. Not every disciple of Jesus is asked to be a leader or evangelist. In fact, most are called to keep life's routines going while allowing a relative few to go walkabout at someone else's expense.

This should make us read the Bible differently, looking out for the unsung heroes and heroines and spotting the details and omissions most people simply read over. While it might be challenging and encouraging for us to hear about the response of

James and John and Simon and Andrew, it might be even more instructive and relevant for us to think through the ramifications of their actions and think about what discipleship meant for those who paid the price. What, for example, of Simon's wife? Or James and John's mother or siblings?

This is not a trivial point. Many Christians feel a sense of perpetual inadequacy in the light of the glory stories they are fed about the extraordinary commitment and service of a few, extrapolating from these that they too should be Christian 'stars'. We all need to be released from this shallow reading of Scripture and the silliness of the usual diet of 'testimonies' offered by some preachers and some publishers.

Zebedee should be as instructive as his sons as we contemplate our own response to the call of Jesus to be disciples of his, hearing the good news of God in the world, seeing everything differently in the light of this, and then getting on with life as people whose ordinary routine might be maintained, but whose life within it is transformed.

Who will dedicate the next new church to be built 'The Church of *Saint* Zebedee'?

Lord God, you call us in different ways to different forms of discipleship in your world. Help us to discern the right response to your call, not regretting that your call to us differs from your call to others. Help us to be faithful wherever your call takes us and whatever cost it demands of us. Amen.

TUESDAY (LENT 1)

MARK 2:13–17   LEVI

IF the name Zebedee evokes memories of a children's TV programme, a single mention of the name Levi will ubiquitously be assumed these days to refer to a make of jeans. Sad, but true. However, Mark specifically records Jesus' encounter with Levi in order to illustrate a very powerful point – in fact, a point that resonates closely with what was said yesterday about the father of James and John. It is simply this: we are supposed to be surprised (if not shocked) by which sorts of people heard and saw the good news of God in Jesus himself. It appears that those who had been most likely to welcome God among them were precisely those who missed him when he came because he didn't tick all the right religious boxes. Their understanding of their Scriptures – particularly in respect of who God was for – led them to expect something or someone different from what they got in Jesus of Nazareth. But those who sinned their boots off and had got used to being regarded as 'unclean' or unsuitable by the orthodox religious establishment found that God was for them … and they had parties to celebrate whenever and wherever they found Jesus.

Levi is a collaborator with an oppressive colonial occupying military force. He is not a popular man with the ordinary people, whose humiliation he feeds by taking their money to maintain and service the imperial Roman system. In one sense this was an indirect connection, because the taxes collected by Levi as people passed from one territory to another probably went directly to Herod Antipas in the first place. But the whole system was deeply resented by ordinary people, and those who serviced it – however reluctantly – were despised. So, Levi is an outcast from polite society and not trusted by anyone.

Experience teaches people like this that they can only expect rejection and hatred. The future would not look bright, because nobody would ever forget that you made your living on the back of their suffering. So, what would be 'good news' to someone like Levi? What might penetrate the cynicism of his own expectations sufficiently to awake in him a spark of hope or of joy?

We read that Jesus was accompanied by a great crowd of people as he taught them while they walked beside the lake. Mark doesn't tell us what he was teaching the people, so we must assume it was variations around the dominant theme of 'good news' and the need for people to see differently and believe what they now saw. The text reads almost as if Jesus decided to illustrate what he was teaching by 'enfleshing' it in a particular person, letting people see what 'hearing good news' and seeing differently ('repenting') might look like when translated from an idea into flesh and blood and spirit. So, he calls over to Levi and invites him to join the party. It was probably to everybody's surprise (and, perhaps, horror) that Levi got up, left his tax booth (and, presumably, his money) and joined the crowd walking with Jesus.

This raises a number of intriguing possibilities for us. While the orthodox religious people don't see what is happening in their midst, an outcast like Levi does.

Jesus is welcomed and embraced by those who have been told endlessly that they do not 'belong', that God is not 'for' them, that God is not on their side, that God can be relied upon to disregard the value of those who do not conform. Levi is an outsider in this world who finds that he is an insider in Jesus' company.

And this is what we will find as we read this gospel: those who ought to 'see' do not, while those who ought to be disqualified from 'seeing' do. It is the upside-down world of God's kingdom where the meek are exalted, the poor hear good news and the powerful find themselves challenged by what sounds to them like very bad news indeed.

But perhaps the most striking element of Levi's experience is that, in common with all those who choose to follow Jesus, he becomes part of a new company, a new community of people who are just beginning to see God and the world differently and who will travel this unknown path together towards a destiny not yet remotely conceivable. Levi is accepted into a group of people who learn that they are enjoying a new start in life, but not alone or in splendid individual isolation. He is learning that you cannot be a follower of Jesus on your own; you automatically become part of a community of people whose only common link is that they are walking in company with Jesus. Levi does not choose his companions any more than they chose him. He might be uncomfortable company, not least because of the way in which his reputation might taint the rest of the group in the eyes of those who don't yet understand what is happening here. But Levi discovers – as presumably do the other followers – that Jesus releases people from their imprisonment by reputation and gives them a new start ... even if the religiously self-righteous find this distasteful.

Surely this must say something to us today about how the Church should be. When one group of Christians tells another that they are unwelcome because of their apparent uncleanness, this story should leap up and embarrass them. It is Jesus who chooses his followers, and it is not up to other disciples to decide for Jesus who may or may not come along. Furthermore, Jesus doesn't ask Levi (any more than he did Simon, Andrew, James or John) to prove his theological credentials before eating with him and sharing his hospitality. No, Jesus takes him as he is and allows him the grace to serve Jesus as he is.

It is relatively easy in our imaginative reading of this text to stand alongside Jesus laughing at the scribes of the Pharisees who are missing the point of it all; but we might do better to stand with them first and hear the words of Jesus afresh with all their challenge to self-righteousness: 'I have come to call not the righteous but sinners'.

Which am I? Which are we in our church? With whom would this Jesus feel most comfortable sharing food, drink and time?

Lord God, whose Son Jesus came to save those who know their need and have no illusions about their weakness, grant grace to those who have heard that you are not for them that they might hear and see afresh. May your church become increasingly a place of welcome and hospitality, reflecting the priorities of the One whose body it purports to be. Amen.

WEDNESDAY (LENT 1)

MARK 3:7–19   THE TWELVE

WORD is spreading about Jesus. He is not all talk, but demonstrates the reality of his words with action. How do people encounter the 'good news' and learn to 'see differently'? They see people being healed, demonic influence being neutralised, disordered lives reordered and unlikely people being included in the company of Jesus' friends.

But all this brings with it a major problem. There is only one Jesus, but there are hundreds of needy people hungry to hear and touch good news. So, Jesus has a choice: either he can trust only himself and just do what he can, driven probably by a sense of his own unique competence and charisma, or he can take the massive risk of bringing other immature, ignorant, untried and untested companions into commission. Fortunately, unlike many religious leaders before and since, Jesus is not an ego-driven prima donna.

The symbolism of this episode is rich and evocative. Jesus is out in the hill country, the place where insurgents and would-be messiahs go to plot their coups. So, Jesus is now putting together the group that will be allied to the true King of Israel, God's anointed, and will become a community that subverts the status quo without using violence as a weapon. Jesus then goes up a mountain – reminiscent of Moses, the deliverer

31

of Israel in the exodus from captivity in Egypt, who went up a mountain to meet with God and receive the Ten Commandments. Jesus then calls to himself a group from the crowd of followers, takes them aside and of them chooses twelve to be commissioned for particular responsibility. Jews had long hoped for and awaited the time when the twelve tribes of Jacob would be resurrected (ten of them had disappeared under Assyrian invasion and subsequent exile) – and now the implicit allusion in Jesus' action is that that very time has come.

There is a feature of this text, however, which might make us pause once again. According to Mark, Jesus 'called to him those whom he wanted' (3:13) … then appointed twelve 'to be with him and to be sent out to proclaim the message …' (3:14). Might this not imply that Jesus called more than twelve, then of them chose the twelve? What, I would like to know, happened to the others? Again, this might be pushing the text too far; but it is too easy for us today to focus only on the 'chosen few' and ignore all the others who, presumably, exercised their discipleship of Jesus in less dramatic ways, but in ways that were acceptable to Jesus. Not everybody (thank God) can be a Simon or a Judas. Most followers of Jesus just get on with life where they are and don't get special mentions in biographies of 'great' Christians.

The twelve, however, are called for two purposes: firstly, they are 'to be with Jesus'; secondly, they are 'to be sent out to proclaim the message, and to have authority to cast out demons'. The dynamic this represents is significant: the twelve must first be captivated by Jesus, watch, listen to and learn from him. They must have the lens behind their eyes – through which they see God, the world and themselves

– reground, enabling them to see as Jesus sees. Thus the people they encounter will hold no fear, for they will be perceived as those who hear 'the message' as either good news or bad news.

However, it is important to recognise that this 'regrinding of the lens behind the eyes' takes time. It doesn't happen instantly. It involves a process of seeing, misinterpreting and misunderstanding, learning, making mistakes and so on. But Jesus does not have the luxury of sending these guys off to theological college for a few years to get trained up; rather, he recognises that people learn to see differently by doing as well as hearing. Being engaged in ministry might be risky on the part of Jesus, but it will allow these rookie apostles to learn on the job.

It is also significant of how Jesus sees that he commits to the twelve precisely the same task that he has been fulfilling since he emerged from the desert and began to proclaim the good news of God that involves repenting (seeing differently) and believing (committing oneself to) the good news. They are not given a subsidiary task which, if it goes wrong, will only cause minimal or incidental damage; no, they are committed with the treasure of Jesus' message and sent out to get on with it. They are not just to talk about it but are to demonstrate the power of its reality in delivering people from their captivity to destructive spirits and the evil that dehumanises. If I had been in Jesus' position, I wouldn't have taken the risk. Thank God Jesus did.

These observations are worthy of serious reflection. How are we to hold together the priorities of 'being with Jesus' (and what might that look like for us today?) and 'being sent out to proclaim the message'? It is worth asking whether or not many contemporary Christians and, indeed, Christian leaders have been close enough to Mark's Jesus to be fully gripped and transformed by the 'message'. For example, do our churches reflect the priorities of God in Jesus by subverting the dominant cultures (even theological and ecclesiastical cultures) with the good news of God's presence; or do they simply assume the normality of the dominant cultures and 'baptise' them? Does a church which plays to the power-hunger and ego of certain charismatic leaders do justice to the nature of Jesus' call and message, or does it simply use Jesus as a vehicle for their own success?

What is clear from this passage is that Jesus calls all sorts of people to go with him. To some he gives particular responsibility, but that does not in any way devalue those who do not lead. Those who are called to exercise special responsibility will have to learn and must be forgiven their failings, for the whole business involves serious watching and listening and doing. Authority is given by Jesus and must be received by the ones who are called in this way; authority can never simply be assumed. That is why any such ministry must be clothed in humility and unafraid of risk – even the risk that we will get the whole thing wrong.

These disciples are beginning a journey that will take them to some difficult places. They have no idea what lies ahead of them, and that is probably just as well. For any person who recognises in Jesus the presence of God and hears a message of good news demanding a new way of seeing and living will embark on a journey of grace and mercy, of risk and failure. There is no room on this journey for the self-righteous or the arrogant.

Lord God, give us the grace to hear your call to us – whether to particular ministry or to everyday discipleship in the ordinary things of life. Help us to have the humility to walk with you in the company of other unlikely companions as we learn and grow and proclaim the message. Amen.

THURSDAY (LENT 1)

MARK 3:16–19 NAME-CHANGES

MARK'S gospel is best read – as is the whole of the Bible – with a very curious mind. The text should tease our imagination and constantly be making us ask questions. And it is often in a mere detail, or what is not being stated overtly, that we find intriguing space for rumination and reflection. Most people, for example, will simply read the narrative of the calling of the twelve apostles and assume that Mark is being neatly pedantic in giving us the names of the lucky men. But this is to miss something remarkable about the names themselves and the experience (or changed way of 'seeing') that lies behind Mark's record.

Simon, we read (3:16), has his name changed by Jesus to Peter. James and John are given a nickname, Sons of Thunder (3:17). Why?

The Bible is full of stories of people who have an encounter with the living God that changes them or sets them off on a new journey in a new direction. Abram (Genesis 12) solemnly hears God's call and promise and becomes Abraham. His wife, Sarai, hears of the part she shall play in this saga and bursts out laughing – probably the response Abram should have had too. (After all, an old man with a childless old wife being told that he will become the father of the nations and that through him all peoples shall be blessed should probably have found the news at least faintly ridiculous.) Sarai becomes Sarah because she was full of laughter and realised that nothing is impossible with God. Jacob becomes Israel after a night of wrestling with an angel at Penuel (Genesis 32) – his new name meaning 'he strove with God and with man, and prevailed'.

Is it not heartening that God honours with a name-change a woman who laughed at him and a man who fought with him … and won? What does this say to those Christians who think God has to be protected from what we really think and experience and be told instead (and repeatedly in songs) that we love him anyway? Should we not learn from the experience of Sarah and Israel that sometimes God expects us to laugh in his face and give him a fight? Doesn't this reinforce the consistent message of the Bible that what God really hates is hypocrisy, complacency and pretence? How many clergy or preachers would still have a job if they encouraged their congregations to laugh and fight?

As we move into the New Testament, we find the same thing happening. Jesus does what God does and plays with people's names. Simon becomes Peter and nobody is supposed to laugh? Peter comes from *petros*, the rock. But the story of this man will go on to show that he is more limestone than granite and that people might have been forgiven for thinking that Jesus was being ironic when he made this particular name-change. Yet isn't that the whole point? Jesus sees the potential for what Simon might become, in time, and portrays the future possibility as a present reality – just as he is also doing in proclaiming that the 'future' coming of God among them is actually now a reality here, even though it will take time for this to be perceived. And maybe Peter is made of porous, leaky limestone, but that is all right in Jesus' eyes; he is consciously calling as one of his main men one who is notoriously fickle and impetuous.

If the point isn't clear enough by now, let's ram it home: Jesus calls people like Simon and me and you, takes us as we are without illusion or pretence, sees what we might become, and gives us a name that shows promise, even if it looks ridiculous to the watching world and those who know us best. Now, isn't that encouraging?

James and John are given a nickname. The sons of Zebedee are to be known as the 'Sons of Thunder'. Now, this might well be ironic and intended to puncture the loud self-confidence of the two brothers. Nothing else is said beyond the actual renaming to enlighten us any further. But, as their story continues, we will see more of the bluster and misguided understanding of these two as they get the wrong end of Jesus' theological stick.

Jesus does not call *special* people to follow him. Nor does he call special (and specially holy) people to join his inner circle. He chooses ordinary people who bring with them all their strengths and weaknesses, their foibles and inconsistencies, their character flaws and limited understandings, and he sees their potential. He looks beyond appearances to the reality within a person and nurtures their confidence by affirming what little they can offer at a particular time and place. He does not despise Simon for not being more of a Peter right now. He doesn't reject the Sons of Thunder because of their personality problems and the danger they might pose to the whole enterprise. Consistent with God's way in the Old Testament narratives, he warms to those who take him seriously enough to be curious enough to leave some things behind in order to see what he is about. He is unafraid of being laughed at or fought with, and chooses people who have the potential to learn humility ... eventually. He takes a long-term view and runs a big risk.

The names we give to our children in the western world do not hold the same significance that they did in Semitic cultures then or, indeed, in Africa or Asia today. In this gospel, the name a person has says something about their person and personality, the hopes their parents might have for them. Jesus demonstrates how names matter in so far as they speak of the potential beyond or behind the apparent, the reality behind the front. In other words, he takes us as we are and sees what we might become ... while still being 'me'. Contrary to the implied theology of some contemporary worship songs, perhaps Jesus wants us not to be 'more like him' but to be more like the person he sees us to be. This is not about losing ourselves but about finding our true selves in our encounter and subsequent journey with Jesus and the ragbag of saints and sinners who walk with him.

Lord God, thank you for choosing people like us to be followers of Jesus. Help us to hear the names you have chosen for us, that we might in turn allow others the possibility of a new name and a new future. Amen.

FRIDAY (LENT 1)

MARK 3:19   WHY JUDAS ISCARIOT?

IF Jesus was so clever, why did he choose as one of his close circle a man with the potential to blow the whole project apart? Why didn't he leave Judas Iscariot as one of the followers whose role was to get on with ordinary life, and not bring him into a place of special responsibility? Did Jesus make a big (and ultimately costly) mistake, or did he have a secret death-wish from the beginning which would then imply a suicidal motivation to Jesus' behaviour? The answers to these questions matter enormously.

Mark did not have to add to Judas's name the phrase 'who betrayed him'. Presumably he did so in order to make some point that might have been missed had he omitted it. As we have already noted, Mark does not waste words. He might simply be sticking the knife into Judas and scoring a point against his memory. But, alternatively, he might be making it clear that we must not forget that the man whose name had by now become synonymous with treachery, blasphemy and betrayal had been deliberately chosen by Jesus at the beginning of his public ministry and specifically included in the core group of disciples. In other words, we are not to demonise Judas Iscariot, but rather to recognise that Jesus saw in him the same potential he saw in Simon, the Sons of Thunder and the others.

In a moment, we will take the time to reflect on Judas Iscariot himself; but first it might be helpful to say something about Mark and his telling of this whole story. In churches today, we read and listen to the reading of the Bible in public worship in an atmosphere of reverent respect. Whatever the content of the passage read, we (at least in the Anglican tradition) respond with the same phrase each time: 'This is the word of the Lord – Thanks be to God'. We are not generally encouraged to respond with a loud 'You must be joking!' or an incredulous 'What on earth was that about?' The effect of this can be to anaesthetise us to the potent, shocking nature of much of what we read and hear from the Scriptures. We are not encouraged generally to ask awkward questions of the text or to do a Jacob/Israel and fight with it. We laugh at the Bible at our peril, despite the experience of Sarai/Sarah.

Mark does not intend his audience to simply sit and absorb his words in a passive state of indifference. He expects us to get up and challenge what we hear, to question it and dig into it. He wants us to stop the reader and interject with a 'Hang on a minute, why did he say *that*?' or a snort of 'Is he really serious?' So, when we read his explanatory identifier ('who betrayed him'), we are supposed to shout out the questions this phrase evokes: Why did he have to add that there? Why did Judas Iscariot betray Jesus, when it all seemed to be starting so well? How did Judas betray Jesus, and what happened between now and then to make betrayal a possibility or an option? Why did Jesus choose this guy if he is such a risk – or didn't Jesus know what he was really like (thus implying that he wasn't as all-seeing as we might like to imagine)? If this were a modern pantomime, we would all jump up and hiss at the mention of Judas' name; but then the more sensitive would become uncomfortable at the swift and implied simplistic judgement that might turn out (as the story progresses) to be a little more complex after all.

I think Mark adds this phrase in order to make us stop and ask questions. He is pointing forward and asking his audience to keep a big question mark above any judgements they make as the story develops. But he might also be drawing attention to the company that Judas Iscariot is keeping. Simon who becomes Peter the rock will deny even knowing Jesus and thereby not exactly cover himself with glory. Thomas (although Mark omits this detail in his resurrection accounts) will question the authenticity of the resurrection. When Jesus hung on the cross, it appears his friends were occupied elsewhere; only several women watched from a distance. When two of Jesus' friends told the others of their encounter with the risen Christ, the others didn't believe a word of it (chapter 16).

So, we see that Judas is in good company. And, if we are going to question Jesus' judgement in choosing Judas in the first place, we will have to raise serious questions about all the others, too. It doesn't look like a very glorious story is going to develop from this intriguing beginning, does it?

Perhaps Mark's point is this: Jesus chose fragile people whose passions and frailties could send them in one of many different directions. But God has chosen to call people like me and you and Peter and Judas and Thomas, fully cognisant of the potential for glory or ruin. This doesn't stop him running the risk of calling people who show signs of being both true and treacherous, strong and weak, committed and complacent.

It is impossible to overstate this element of the gospels – and especially that of Mark. Discipleship, even for those called to leadership and responsibility, is an unwritten book; there is no blueprint to follow that will guarantee a particular end. Jesus calls people simply to start out with him on the journey and see what happens as they go. There is the potential for amazing change; but there is also the possibility of great disaster. And it is often the same person who produces both. Christians should neither elevate their leaders onto pedestals of unrealistic holiness or consistency, nor fantasise that there is a stage of discipleship where everything becomes safe and predictable.

Mark invokes Judas and his motley group of passionate companions in order to tell us to get real about what it means to follow Jesus in an uncertain world with an uncertain church made up of uncertain people. Thus it has always been, and thus it shall probably always continue to be. So, don't continue to read this gospel narrative if you prefer the security of fantasy – even religious or theological fantasy.

Lord God, preserve us from seeking safety in mock-sanctity. Grant us the courage to be honest about ourselves and one another, recognising that you know what we are like, from where we have come, and what we might become ... or not. Amen.

SATURDAY (LENT 1)

MARK 3:20–35   JESUS' FAMILY

JESUS cannot shake off the crowds. Even when he goes into a house for rest and food, the people won't go away. When healing has been seen and God seems to be present, no amount of pressure will dissuade the needy and the curious from wanting to see and hear for themselves. But already the threat to Jesus is apparent. The scribes of the Pharisees are people who expect God to work in particular ways and through particular channels (rituals, obedience to specific laws that govern behaviour and define 'belonging' or 'uncleanness'), and they are already finding Jesus irksome because he appears to be breaking the rules. After all, how can God possibly be acting in and through someone who appears not to be according the religious authorities the status, dignity and authority they rightfully enjoy? If Jesus carries on this way, and takes a load of people with him, he might well begin to establish an alternative 'priesthood' or a parallel 'church'.

Therefore, the charge that he must be either in league with the Accuser or possessed by him is not a silly one. What other options are available to people who have a vested interest in seeing Jesus as deeply problematic or even blasphemous? But Jesus responds by affirming his role as the one who is called to be stronger than John the Baptiser and has found that his house (that is, the house that is God's people) is being burgled by those whose role ought to be to protect and serve it. So, Jesus uses an image that will rankle in the imagination of the religious authorities, making them angry that their accusation against him has been taken, reinterpreted and handed back to them in a very direct and upsetting way.

And witnessing all of this is the family of Jesus.

One of the frustrations of reading this gospel is that we sometimes feel we are listening to a one-way conversation – a bit like eavesdropping on someone else's mobile telephone call on a train or a bus. You have to try to work out what the other person is saying in order to make sense of the side of the conversation you *can* hear. Jesus encounters certain people, and we observe their reaction, but then a whole load of questions go unanswered as Mark races on to the next event.

Jesus' family are worried. They think he has gone out of his mind, and they want to take him home for safe keeping. He deals with the scribes (probably much to the embarrassment and horror of his mother and siblings) and then makes an extraordinary – brutal, even – statement about his family to those who are listening and watching him closely. The frustration is that we do not learn how his family responded to this! Mark doesn't tell us. Did they argue with him? Did his mother weep and his brothers accuse him of being heartless? Did they understand what he was on about and simply acquiesce? We don't know, so we can only guess.

But it does raise for us the question behind the immediate text regarding the nature of 'vocation'. Given that Mary, the mother of Jesus, has a special place reserved for her in the Christian tradition, what are we to make of this element in her calling? (This illustrates very well the danger some preachers easily fall into whereby they draw conclusions from a particular text in isolation from the bigger picture which might nuance or even change the possible conclusions.) Clearly, part of the calling for Jesus' family was to go through all the processes of disbelief, embarrassment, social stigma, questioning and relearning. And this was a process in their discipleship that could not be rushed. Instant theological or ethical perfection was not an option. They had to walk this particular path – a path unique to them and open to nobody else.

It could be said that Jesus' family had to learn in a very harsh way that discipleship meant letting go of Jesus and what they wanted him to be in order to see him as he was and to be shaped (ultimately) by that experience. Jesus was inaugurating a new community of people whose belonging together transcends traditional family, ethnic, racial and social bonds. This new 'family' is one which does not reject or denigrate those traditional bonds and relationships (as might be demanded by some cults) but transcends them and, therefore, reshapes them.

None of what follows in the gospel between Jesus and his family will be possible without this experience here. Fundamental to the experience of the early church was this 'letting go' of Jesus before he could be properly understood and followed. It is not too great a leap to imagine that this is an experience that many Christians would benefit from today. We all know of committed Christians who have had to lose their faith and their image of God and Jesus in order later to find them afresh (and different). For such people, their apprehension of Jesus might be one that is not recognised by the gospel accounts of him. I often wonder what the Jesus of the gospels would make of some of the rather wet songs we sing about him in contemporary worship. It is also possible that different images of Jesus are appropriate to different people at different times of life. But Jesus will not allow himself to be tamed or subdued by familiarity or friendliness. He has a habit, as this gospel is already demonstrating, of saying what people don't want to hear, of refusing to be constrained by perceptions or expectations of what he should be like or what he should say and do.

Mary and her children had to walk a hard path in order to follow their calling to be followers of Jesus and not just his mother and family. They had to let go of him and 'lose' him.

They were not the only ones. Discipleship today must surely involve the same.

Lord God, we want – even need – to put Jesus in a box which makes him comfortable and predictable. Preserve us from this urge and lead us on the hard road walked by Mary and her family, letting go of our 'sacred' images in order to find Jesus again. Amen.

PERSONAL REFLECTION

Reflect on your own life story and ask yourself: how did I first hear the call of Jesus to walk with him? What made me say yes? What has been the cost so far … and who has paid it?

GROUP DISCUSSION

1. In going on a journey, we have to leave some things behind. What have we left behind (as individuals or as a church?) as a consequence of following Jesus?

2. Am I called to be a James/John or a Zebedee? In what ways can we make space for others to become followers of Jesus … at a cost to us?

3. Who are the co-followers of Jesus whom you would prefer he had *not* called to join us on the journey?

4. What would it look like for us to 'be with Jesus'?

HEALINGS

SUNDAY (LENT 2)

MARK 1:21–45 A WOMAN AND A LEPER

SOME people are all talk and no action. We are all rightly suspicious of people who make great claims but never provide evidence of that which they claim so boldly. We become easily weary of people who are good at 'talking the talk' but never seem to 'walk the walk'. Conversely, we often want to hear a verbal explanation of what we have seen somebody do and why they did it. Words and actions have to go together: without words, actions might be inexplicable or misunderstood; without actions, words might seem empty. In his gospel, Mark is clear that Jesus holds together words and actions with an authority that commands attention.

We remember that, following his baptism, Jesus began his public ministry by returning to Galilee and proclaiming the good news of God, calling people to repentance and belief (a new way of seeing and commitment to this perspective). He gave to those whom he called to go with him the authority to proclaim the good news (that God is among them again) and to demonstrate it by bringing healing and wholeness to broken lives and restoring order to those whose personalities had been taken over by destructive forces. Jesus, we note, did not reserve for himself this task of demonstrating the truth of words by healing action, but risked letting his friends have that same authority.

But Mark has selected his material carefully. He hasn't just thrown together some random examples or illustrations to pad the text out a bit. Rather, he immediately takes us from the calling of the first disciples on the beach to the ministry of public teaching (on the Sabbath) and healing. Mark does not want to waste time on great discourses and theological reflection; he wants to go straight for the action – for that is what, in his eyes, made Jesus so fantastically popular among people who needed healing and restoration, and so hugely threatening to those who thought they did not. Mark wants his audience to engage immediately with the behaviour of Jesus and ask some pretty fundamental questions. If we are the sort of sceptical people who hear of heaven's affirmation of Jesus at his baptism in the Jordan, hear John the Baptiser's identification of him, and see him coming along proclaiming the good news of God's presence, we might justly ask where the evidence is to be found to demonstrate that Jesus isn't just another tinpot messiah, another charlatan and fraud. We will know from our Scriptures (Isaiah 61, for example) that God's servant will bring good news and demonstrate it in freeing captives, healing the sick, restoring sight to those who cannot see. So, that is probably what we are going to be looking for in anyone who claims to be 'anointed by the Spirit to proclaim good news'. Mark takes us there without any fuss at all. Let the words take flesh as people are healed and disorder is ordered.

First of all, Jesus tackles the powers of disordered darkness that enslave people and destroy their lives and personalities. We do not know what has gone on in this man's life except that he is in the synagogue (therefore ritually clean?) and reacts strongly to Jesus' words and presence. Jesus silences him (would that he would silence more people in today's churches!) and brings wholeness through a violent convulsion. Restoration does not come easily or comfortably; it comes messily.

But the interesting feature here is that the witnesses of this event remark primarily on the authority with which Jesus teaches ... and endorses that teaching with action that vindicates the teaching. They are primarily amazed not at the deliverance from demonic influence but at what the whole business says about *who* Jesus is and by what authority he can behave in this way. Again, the actions of Jesus are supposed in the first instance to make us ask questions about Jesus, his identity and claims, followed by our response. Do we 'see differently' and commit ourselves to the truth that we witness, or do we find ourselves entertained by novelty and excitement and take it no further?

Jesus then goes on to heal Simon's mother-in-law. Why is this significant? Well, though it might sound a bit obvious, she is a woman. A woman is of little account in that culture, and she should be serving the men. Jesus heals her and restores her where others would have disregarded her.

After dealing with all sorts of other people, Jesus decides to get away for some peace and quiet where he can pray. Again he is followed and decides to take his friends to other villages to proclaim the good news there also. His mission is very clear, and it has not changed from the simple statements of 1:15. But, of all the many people whom Jesus healed in the course of these journeys through the villages and towns of Galilee, why does Mark expand specifically on these three: the demonically influenced man, the mother-in-law of Simon, and now the leper? Well, if we haven't grasped it before now, the story of the leper's encounter with Jesus will force the point home. God's presence, recognised in words and actions of healing and renewal, is experienced by those who might well be regarded as outsiders, those in some way seen as 'unclean'.

Surely the presence of God is to be seen first by priests and prophets and scribes of the Pharisees? Surely it is they, the religious professionals who study the Scriptures and know the signs, who will recognise the presence of God among them when he comes in power? Well, apparently not so. Mark makes it clear that it is a disordered man, a mere woman and a feared and outcast leper who hear and see and touch the good news of God and find new life, new dignity, a new place among the people of God, a new community of God's renewed people, a new way of seeing and living.

Mark is just beginning to tell us that this gospel is full of scandalous surprises and outrageous generosity. The tragedy, of course, is that those who should have recognised him did not.

Is there not a warning here even today: that those of us who feel we 'know' Jesus are in greatest danger of missing him when he comes among us and touches all the 'wrong' people?

Lord God, Jesus was received by unusual people, but by people who knew their need. Set us free from our pride that we might not be numbered among those who miss your coming because you don't look like we think you should. Amen.

MONDAY (LENT 2)

MARK 2:1–12 A PARALYTIC MAN

FOR Mark, there is no let-up in the action. Having witnessed the deliverance of a demonically influenced man, the healing of Simon's mother-in-law and the restoration of a leper, Jesus goes home. Yes, he goes to *his* home. And there he finds no peace either, because the crowds just will not give up. They find out where he is and, like fans surrounding the hotel where a pop star is holed up, they won't go until they have seen him.

Now this is interesting, not only for the encounter between the lawyers and Jesus, but because the hole in the roof is probably a hole cut into Jesus' own roof. Secondly, it is the faith of the paralysed man's friends and not the man's own faith that leads to forgiveness. Thirdly, we discover that forgiveness and healing go hand in hand for this man. No wonder it caused a scandal among the religious experts and professionals. What we have here is a subversion of received religious orthodoxy and a visible and stark challenge to the powers of disorder, chaos, sickness … and to the bad news that destruction always wins, that injustice always triumphs, that the world cannot be changed, that death always has the last word. Furthermore, this episode also challenges the notion that individuals respond to God and receive his grace in isolation from other individuals by having a man healed on the basis of his friends' faith and as a member of a community.

Mark is interested in driving home his point that Jesus is exercising authority in a way that brings together heaven and earth. God's anointed assumes the power to forgive sins *and* to make a person well. In one sense, this is figurative of what needs to happen to Israel, the whole people of God. Their exile needs to come to an end – indeed, has come to an end with the arrival of Jesus on the scene proclaiming the good news of God – and they need to be healed. This healing means seeing and living differently within their current circumstances, not necessarily being delivered from them. In other words, the people can remain under the jackboot of the Roman Empire but be liberated within themselves as a people who cannot be held down by an earthly power. For God has set them free to be no longer prisoners – whatever the Emperor in Rome might have to say about it.

But what is equally significant here is the role of the wider community of God's people in the healing of this particular man and what that might say to us. It is not clear whether this paralysed man was brought willingly or resentfully to see Jesus. Mark doesn't tell us if he was reluctant or grateful. We have no idea if it was his idea in the first place or that of his friends. Was this an act of love on their part, or were they fed up with his moaning about his lot in life? Did they want him to be 'economically active' again instead of 'sponging' off others? We don't know because we aren't told. So, we tend to use our imagination to set the assumptions with which we then fill out the story. And so be it.

However, we can be sure of some things. Whatever the story and however they came to be there, these friends carried the paralysed man, dug a hole in

Jesus' roof and got round the obstructive crowd that way. They were persistent, to say the least. They knew that Jesus could make a difference to this man's life, and they weren't going to miss the opportunity. They presumably could have been doing something else with their time, or they could have observed due etiquette and left the roof intact. But, instead, they used their ingenuity and determination, acted together with optimism and faith, chose to push their case (something Jesus seems constantly to admire in people who are bothered enough to be persistent nuisances), and made sure they saw the job through. Again, we don't know how they responded to the whole business or what they did afterwards. We are just given a snapshot to serve Mark's primary purpose.

But surely this says something to us about the nature of God's people being persistent in bringing others to Jesus – whether they like it or not? Isn't there something here about healing being found where God's people refuse to give up on their friends and then act together in sacrificial service, not for their own benefit but for the healing and well-being of someone else?

Here, indeed, is a sign of the presence of God among his people. Friends are compelled to act together on the basis of their own commitment and for the sake of someone else who might not even deserve to be taken so seriously. Jesus forgives the man (and his friends for messing up his roof?), argues with the lawyers and sends him on his way to become an active member of society – not the passive one he has been accustomed to being thus far.

Yet the tragedy again is that the people who should know better completely miss the point. They turn the pastoral reality of this man's plight into a theological

Jesus keeps coming and answering their prayers by his presence, his words and his actions.

The problem is: they can't see it. It is as though they have been told a good joke repeatedly for years but are awaiting the punchline. But, when it comes, they are too deaf to hear it, too inured by silence (or the repetition of the joke) to be ready for it or open to its possibility. So, they don't get the joke because they never hear the punchline.

Once again, then, on the Sabbath, Jesus comes to the synagogue and realises the games that people are playing with him. He should not be 'working' on the Sabbath, and to heal people is obviously 'work' in the minds of those who are already out to get him. Jesus is not a shrinking violet; he is perfectly content to upset the religiously self-righteous who mistake the form for the reality to which it points. The Sabbath 'rest' is intended to reflect God's rest after the labour of creation and his deliverance of his people from their slavery in Egypt at the Exodus. For a suffering people, it points ahead to the day of God's deliverance and keeps alive the people's hopes for the future of the people. But this symbol, this pause in the relentless routine of life, has been turned into a weapon of control, a symbol of the game-playing in which religious people can so easily engage. The focus was now upon 'scoring' people's righteousness and either including or excluding them accordingly. Elaborate systems of criteria had been developed to identify what was allowable and what was not when it came to obeying the letter of the law. It was permitted to walk a certain distance on the Sabbath, but not one metre more. It would be a bit like saying you are a saint if you walk a mile with your dog by your side, but a sinner if you walk the same distance with your dog on a leash.

One can't help thinking that giving so much attention to the minutiae of working out such criteria is really a sort of distraction therapy for people who have lost the plot. The detail subverts the big picture and diverts the observer into unnecessary and futile religious and legal nitpicking.

The big picture looks something like this. God created all that is. As he went about the business of creation, he kept looking at what he had made and loved it to bits. He is almost playful in his inventiveness and embarrassingly excited by the results. The Sabbath ordinance is partly meant to compel the observer to remember the playful grace of the God in whose image we are created. The Sabbath is intended not as a punishment or a tool by which authorities can establish a scale for judging the righteousness of individuals or communities; rather, it is a time to remember and relive what God did and does: he creates and plays and enjoys the fruits of his labour. In other words, the Sabbath is a living reminder of God's grace and liberating love. It is not a legal mechanism for stopping people doing things.

This all becomes starkly visible and unavoidably embarrassing when Jesus heals the man with a withered hand. Is not the day of God's creation and grace precisely the day when God's healing and delivering power should be exercised and seen to be real? Is not healing the work of God himself – and, therefore, those who are made in his image and called to reflect his nature and grace? Is not the Sabbath precisely the right day for blowing away legalistic religious nonsense and setting people free from their bondage to such imprisonments? Is not the Sabbath the perfect day for religious people (who claim to know God and know about him) to let go of the idols they set up to distract them from the reality of God's call? Surely, if the Sabbath is to be for any purpose whatsoever, it must be for this: to set God's people free to enjoy the creation, to relish the fruit of God's grace, to enjoy God and his world, and to rejoice at taking the time to see what God is doing – even when he seems to be breaking his own rules.

I guess that the man who used to have a withered hand had little difficulty in recognising the healing grace of God that takes priority over the legalistic obsessions of religious powermongers and those who can't see the presence and activity of God when it hits them between the eyes.

Lord God, you have created all things and made us in your image. Set your people free – especially those who make the rules – to enjoy your creative love, to identify the fruits of your joyful labour, and to allow the space for all your children to see your face and feel your healing touch. Amen.

WEDNESDAY (LENT 2)

Mark 5:1–20   The demoniac

Sometimes, what happens to an individual seems to speak (for those who have the ears to hear or the eyes to see) of a wider phenomenon, perhaps representing the fate of a whole group of people or a nation. For example, a footballer scores yet another own goal, and this is reported as somehow epitomising the haplessness of the whole disaster-prone team. Or the apparently targeted murder of a gay man on London's South Bank is seen to represent the victimisation of the wider gay community by people full of prejudice and hate. Or a priest in Communist Poland is tortured and killed, thus becoming a symbol of the suffering of a people under cruel oppression, but a people whose voice would not be silenced ... even by a lonely death at the hands of men who thought they could get away with it.

When Jesus leaves the Jewish areas and walks among the Gentiles in the region of the Ten Towns, what happens to him is to be understood at different levels, speaking of both the particular engagement with one man and his community and the plight of the Jewish people in general.

The 'demoniac' has three things (at least) going against him: firstly, he lives among the graves of the dead; secondly, he lives in close proximity to pigs;

thirdly, he is excluded from civil society because of his obsessions and mania. To a Jewish mind, living among the dead makes you unclean. Pigs are unclean animals and they defile a Jew, making him 'dirty' and excluded from the community of faith and the religious rites and rituals that represent who they are before their God. This man is an outcast ... and a Gentile to boot. In Jewish eyes, he doesn't have a lot going for him.

When Jesus comes across him, he is ranting and raving, hurling abuse and challenging Jesus. He is self-destructive in his mania and strikes fear into those who encounter him. He is in the grip of a malevolent and destructive power which will not let him go, from which he cannot be freed – much as the Jews felt they were in the grip of the evil imperial Roman occupying powers. Jesus, in whom the presence and kingdom of God is incarnated, comes into this place, and the challenge is on: will the evil powers that grip both Israel and individuals win over the power of God's anointed, the one called to fulfil Israel's calling? Will the powers, stripped naked in their destructive violence, now do violence to Jesus?

What is interesting here is that Jesus doesn't keep away from what is deemed unclean or impure. He walks among the Gentiles, close to the pigs, and engages with a powerful and outcast man. He doesn't walk away or demand that his world be kept immune from such people. He chooses to go (although the reason for his digression into this territory is unclear) into the unclean place where he might become contaminated by others not like him.

Jesus throws out the obsessive and oppressive powers and sets the man free to take his place in his society again. He sets him free in the same place where he was previously trapped. And the deliverance of the man becomes a sort of representation, a symbolic prefiguring, of the deliverance of God's people from the destructive and violent hands of their oppressors. The rule of God, personified in Jesus, will do away with the seemingly indestructible forces of empire. As this huge herd of swine – all 2,000 of them – run dementedly into the sea, so will Rome one day see itself destroyed. For power, built on a foundation of cruelty and injustice, will not ultimately prevail. However invincible the prevailing systems appear to be, their time will come. God will not be mocked – and imperialism, with all its death and horrors, will not have the last word.

But there is a further element to this story, one that Mark wants to drop into the (sub)consciousness of the audience. Jesus himself will one day be cast out from the community to a place where he will be flayed with the stones of Roman whips. There he will be regarded as unclean and will take into himself the powerful destructiveness of this world – all that humanity can possibly throw at him – and be cast into a sea of death. This Jesus will take upon himself the horrors of a world gone mad and will bear in his own flesh the unjust punishment visited upon a herd of swine. But, by this apparent defeat and humiliation, those who have been oppressed by destructive powers and dehumanising forces will find themselves healed and restored, clothed and human once again. The echoes of this episode will resonate when Calvary looms and the audience will try to make sense of what they are hearing or reading.

It is interesting that this man wants to stay in the company of Jesus, going with him and enjoying the security of being close to the source of his healing. But Jesus refuses to let him do this. The one who has experienced the healing power of God is called then to leave Jesus and take his own responsibility for telling his story and bearing witness to what has happened. Jesus did not call everybody to exercise discipleship in the same way. As we have seen already, some are called to accompany him and others are called to let him go. But what is clear is that Jesus will not be pinned down or possessed – even by those who claim to have been most intimately touched by him. Jesus has a nasty habit of telling people to let go of him and take responsibility for their own discipleship.

Mark knows what he is doing here. This wreck of a man is not a Jew, but is acceptable to Jesus. Jesus, once again, breaks the rules and heals the 'wrong' people. Rather than maintain his own purity, he goes to where his own cleanness is most likely to be contaminated. He brings healing and wholeness where these looked to be impossible. He refuses to let healed people hang on to him, but sends them out and away from him. And those who witness all this are either astonished or scared witless. They beg him to leave and go somewhere else.

Jesus was apparently deemed dangerous and unsettling to all sorts of people who thought they had the world (and God) sussed. And nothing seems to have changed, even today.

Lord God, we Christians sometimes become obsessed with maintaining our own purity and excluding those who threaten the same. Open our eyes to the glory of Jesus' lack of fear of contamination. Help us to witness his healing powers – even where we least expect it – and to have the courage to tell our world what we have seen. Amen.

THURSDAY (LENT 2)

MARK 5:21–43   A DAUGHTER AND A WOMAN

IT can sometimes appear that the gospels record a series of disconnected events. However, Mark is keen for us to see how the complex of demands on Jesus reflects the reality of the lives we all lead. Things often do not happen tidily and in order. So, two women – possibly unknown to each other – find that their lives overlap and their stories overlap in Mark's account of Jesus' healing ministry.

Jairus is President of the Synagogue and might be expected to be among those who are at best suspicious of and at worst antagonistic towards Jesus. But, as is the case with many of us, when it is our own flesh and blood who are in desperate need, we override our prejudices and grasp for any straw. Thus it is that Jairus, this important man, approaches Jesus and asks him to help his sick daughter. Jesus responds by setting off, pursued by the crowds, to see the girl. And now the second woman's story interjects and takes over the narrative for a while. Having attended to this woman, Jesus then continues and ministers to Jairus' daughter. But the story is not as straightforward as it might at first seem to be.

This little girl is 12 years old. This woman (of indeterminate age; she might only have been in her mid-twenties) has suffered for twelve years. The little girl's father is fearful – of losing his daughter, but possibly also of the local gossip and stigma that might follow his humiliating appeal to Jesus; the woman is also fearful – of being exposed in front of a judgemental crowd. And yet Jesus shows no fear of possibly being contaminated (again) by contact with a dead body and with a woman whose bodily discharges make her ritually unclean. Are we getting the point Mark is trying to drive home to us? Jesus goes into the places of impurity and exposes his own cleanness to contamination in the name of love and God's healing presence. He does not see the preservation of his own purity as a goal of his mission or calling.

If the Church is called to be the body of this same Jesus and to reflect his nature and behaviour, surely the Christian community should be going into those places shunned by others – even into places and among people that Christians believe to be 'unclean', capable of contaminating the Church. Christians cannot evade the compelling demand of Jesus to get their hands dirty. The Church should surely be less concerned about its own internal purity and should welcome those whose contribution to the Church might turn out to be one of contamination. To follow this Jesus means to risk everything, regardless of the stigma this will inevitably evoke even among other 'more pure' Christians. Here, we recognise that the fear of humiliation within the religious community proves powerless where Jesus is concerned. But that fear should never be underestimated. The Church is no stranger to the accusation of being a judgemental body of holier-than-thou bigots who welcome only those who pass the tests of ethical purity. Perhaps the Church needs to recover the Jesus of this gospel and reread the Scriptures in the light of it.

As we return to the narrative, we find Jesus inviting trust alongside the fear and establishing that his presence brings a confrontation with death and all the destructiveness of the world. It is as if Jesus is putting down markers for what will happen to himself later when on a cross he will confront the violent and dehumanising powers of darkness and defeat them. A little girl finds her life restored; a woman finds her life and dignity reborn. Where stigma and fear once dominated, life and hope now take root. But that is not all that can be said about Mark's purpose in intertwining the predicaments of these two women.

The woman whose bleeding is healed finds that her willingness to risk everything for contact with Jesus opens the way to healing. But this healing, though personal, can never be private. The whole company of people becomes involved in the event, and the woman's healing is not a merely private matter for herself and those close to her. In other words, it is public and open to public scrutiny. Jairus' daughter is restored to life, and the whole community knows about it. The questions these healings evoke cannot be ducked or dealt with on the quiet; rather, they must be talked about and argued over in the public domain.

This also speaks powerfully to the wider Christian community, even today. Christian faith can never be a merely private matter, relegated to the status of permissible opinion. And Christians must not allow questions of faith to be confined to the private 'box', even when it is convenient for the dominant culture to wish to do so. Faith in Jesus is always personal but cannot avoid a public dimension. Claims of healing or theological force must always be open to public scrutiny and run the risk of denial. This is why it is so important that Christian scholars should be supported as they tackle in the universities and colleges the questions many of us would like to avoid having to ask. This is why the job of clergy is frequently to interpret, in a language that is understandable by ordinary people, the openness of God to the world, giving voice to the wrestlings of Christian people with the hard questions of life. Bland quotations of Bible verses do not help when a tsunami wipes out hundreds of thousands of people and the world asks where God was when the waters flooded in.

The passage concludes with a lovely detail. Jesus raises Jairus' daughter from the dead. He doesn't make a song and dance about it or call the press in for a media conference. He doesn't explain himself and draw attention to his immense healing power. No – he asks for the little girl to be fed.

Jesus is the one who is called to proclaim and embody the kingdom, the rule, of God. He heals the sick and raises the dead, thus pointing to what will ultimately be won through his own death and resurrection. But he deals with broken people with straightforward dignity, and he attends to the simple details of their basic humanity. Christians must never separate out the physical from the spiritual, making Jesus more 'spiritual' than he actually is. The face of Jesus will be seen in his people when they give attention to the simple details of ordinary life and hold these as inextricably intertwined with healing and restoration.

Lord God, may your people look to our world and our communities like Jesus looked to his. Give us the grace to meet fear with love, brokenness with healing, death with life. Set us free from our own fear and pride to be a people open to the world, for Christ's sake. Amen.

FRIDAY (LENT 2)

MARK 7:31–7   A DEAF AND MUTE MAN

HAVING noted yesterday that faith can never be private but must always be open to public scrutiny, we now have Jesus taking a man away from the crowds for healing in private. How, then, do we hold these two events together?

One of the notable things about Jesus is his sensitivity to the particular individual with whom he has to do. There is a time for healing and a time for talking about it. This man is a unique individual whose need is for quiet attention from Jesus. Later, although the crowds are instructed to keep quiet about what they had witnessed, this man is given no such order. His healing will be publicly acknowledged, and anyone will be able to discuss it and hold an opinion about it. This ministry is personal and, later, public; though exercised apart from the crowds, it does not remain private between Jesus and the man himself.

The context of this passage is important. Things are soon going to come to a head for Jesus. He is proclaiming the presence of the kingdom of God and demonstrating it in healing broken people, restoring sight and hearing to those who have become used to the bad news of God's punishment. The proclamation of good news is enfleshed and there for all to see. Yet Jesus seems also to want to keep the effects of his ministry under wraps until the time is right for him to confront the authorities in an ultimate showdown. There is a tension here, principally because people cannot keep their mouths shut about what they have seen and heard. More of this later.

A man who is deaf cannot hear good news of any sort. A man who has a severe speech impediment (possibly related to his deafness) cannot speak good news, but simply represents the bad news of brokenness and sadness. Any good Jew would know, however, that the sign of God's kingdom come would be the fulfilment or incarnation of Isaiah's prophecy in 35:5–6, echoed in 61:1–3. These passages speak of the eyes of the blind being opened, the broken-hearted being tended, the 'ears of the deaf unstopped' and 'the mute tongue shout[ing] for joy'. However, the texts do not spell out what the previously deaf will now hear or what the hitherto dumb will now want to shout. The answer comes in Jesus and the good news he proclaims to a broken people in a broken world.

We have to remember that the people of Jesus' time have been suffering the humiliation of occupation by a pagan empire. Every day they wake up, they see before their eyes the fact of God's apparent absence. They cling to the hope that God's silence does not indicate his defeat or absence; but the evidence does not look good. Oppression has been going on in this way for several generations, and there appears to be no end in sight. What, to these people, would sound like good news? Surely that God has not abandoned them and will return to set them free? So, when Jesus comes proclaiming 'good news' and claiming to embody the good news itself – the news of God's presence among them – surely people will be delighted and relieved and celebrate accordingly? Well, not quite. Some people have got used to 'reality', and, despite the hopes they recite in their Scriptures, their actual hope has grown dim. Others have become inured to the present indignities and have become blind to seeing signs of God's presence invading the present. Some can no longer hear good news because they have ceased to expect anything other than misery.

In one sense, this deaf and mute man represents such people. He longs for healing and restoration but can no longer articulate it. He doesn't ask Jesus for healing (how could he?) but wants Jesus to 'touch him'. It is a request for physical touch, human embrace. And Jesus not only accedes to the request, he goes the extra mile in bringing together physical stuff and spiritual need. Healing is not notional, nor is it imaginary. Healing comes by a combination of Jesus and earthly stuff – spit and dirt. Jesus never spiritualises what is essentially physical and never allows people to escape into a spiritual cocoon where they can be protected from the uncomfortable muckiness of the world. Discipleship itself is about flesh and blood, things and stuff, the everyday business of life in a particular place at a particular time. Yet, in this particular place and time, Jesus brings heaven and earth together and demonstrates the presence of the living God here and now.

But we still cannot escape the earlier question: what does this man now hear, and what is it his tongue has been released to shout out? In one sense, the answer is simple: a man who was deaf to the world (and, because of the world, to God?) hears the good news of God's presence; having received healing, he is now to proclaim healing to others whose ears have been dulled to good news. And the hint for all God's people becomes clear: if you have heard the good news and experienced the healing, reconciling presence and love of God in the person and life of Jesus Christ, then you cannot keep quiet about it. It is not a private matter. You are obliged by your experience of God's good grace to share it with others. You, who have begun to 'see' differently, are compelled to describe God, the world and life in such a way that other people glimpse the possibility of seeing and living differently – in other words, repenting.

The crowds who witnessed the effects of Jesus' ministry on this man are told to keep quiet about it; but they can no more do this than stop breathing for a week. Good news cannot be suppressed. Jesus must be disobeyed because this news is not capable of being hidden.

Lord God, who opens our ears to hear good news and our mouths to share it with the world in which we live, keep us faithful to that calling. May our mouths always be open to speak of you in ways that bring healing and the hope of heaven to people who have forgotten what love is all about. And, where the dumb have yet to speak, may your people open their mouths on their behalf. Amen.

SATURDAY (LENT 2)

MARK 10:46–52   A BLIND BEGGAR

IT all looks so straightforward, doesn't it? Jesus and his friends are making their way to Jerusalem, and a blind beggar waylays them. Whereas the crowd finds his interjections to be a real nuisance, a distraction from hearing what Jesus was trying to say, Jesus calls him and asks him what he wants. Jesus heals him, restoring his sight, and they all live happily ever after. Another healing notch to Jesus' credit. Mark's gospel is full of such episodes, and this one is just added in order to emphasise the nature of Jesus' miraculous gifts.

Well, to be satisfied with that is to miss the point Mark is actually wanting to reinforce. To understand the import of it, you have to look back to the passage that immediately precedes this one, 10:32–45, and particularly verse 36. Here, two of Jesus' closest followers tell Jesus they want him to do something for them, and Jesus asks them what this is. Their answer has to do with status, power and privilege. In the episode with the blind beggar that follows, Jesus asks Bartimaeus: 'What do you want me to do for you?' And Bartimaeus, the one cursed with a debilitating infirmity that renders him useless in ordinary society, responds with a clear request for the restoration of his sight. Jesus obliges, noting that the blind man's faith has been the means of his healing/salvation. The understanding of James and John (who have been close to Jesus) is contrasted with that of Bartimaeus (who has never seen him or been acquainted with him). The request of James and John is rejected (in the sense that they intended it in the first place) while the request of Bartimaeus is granted. It is almost as if the blind man could see before he had his sight, whereas the 'seeing' companions of Jesus were actually blind to who Jesus is and what he is about.

This contrast is yet another point of surprise in the gospel. The ones we expect to be 'in' are 'out', and those who might be regarded as 'out' find themselves 'in'. The kingdom of Jesus is subversive of our expectations and challenging to those who claim to be closest to Jesus himself. Being a follower of Jesus does not automatically confer the right to arrogance or righteousness. It seems that it is often those who are closest who are most likely to miss the point, while others who seem to be blind to God and his ways get the point immediately. The only response by those who walk closely with Jesus is one of humility.

However, there is another element in Bartimaeus' experience. When he hears that Jesus of Nazareth is coming, he cries out two things: firstly, he recognises who Jesus is ('Son of David'); secondly, he asks for pity. Perhaps it was this stark openness that made Jesus stop and call Bartimaeus to him. The only qualification for becoming a follower of Jesus is to glimpse who he is and then, in the light of this recognition or identification, to ask for mercy. Bartimaeus knows that his initial need is to receive from God what he cannot achieve for himself. Jesus, the presence of God incarnate, can take him as he is and offer him hope and healing. In other words, the first point of becoming a follower of Jesus is to acknowledge one's need. This is not a weakness, but rather a mark of honesty and courage. It further becomes the levelling point for Jesus' followers: if the only thing they have in common is an acknowledgement of need when faced with the presence of God in Jesus, then the only response is one of naked humility. That is why Christians are in no position to stand in judgement on anyone else.

But there are echoes here of a common problem for the people of God. The Christian community would like to believe that it is a company of people open and welcoming to those who wish to join the journey of common discipleship. Yet the evidence is often the opposite. Bartimaeus calls out and is perceived by the crowds of Jesus' followers as a nuisance, an irritant, a distraction from the real business. Life would clearly be better if Bartimaeus and people like him would just go away and stop bothering Jesus. Some people don't naturally fit in our 'church'; they don't understand how we do things, don't believe the right things or don't articulate them in the right language. They insist on asking awkward questions or don't dress properly. Whatever the case, the image of the 'church' would be better without them; anyway, they will only consume too much time and energy which could be better used in establishing more professional discipleship programmes. But Jesus ignores the protestations of his followers and waits for the 'outsider' who then expresses a more direct and simple faith and grasp of theology than any of the others.

The Church has frequently to stop and ask where we would be in this picture. Are we to be found with the crowd, claiming to be serious followers of Jesus on the road towards Jerusalem, but missing those who cry out from the roadside and rejecting their intrusions as unwelcome distractions? Or are we standing with Jesus, open to learning that his priorities are not the same as ours? Are we willing to recognise that the pursuit of our own discipleship in the company of the Church might be precisely the barrier that prevents from coming to Jesus those whom Jesus sees as a priority?

These are not easy questions to address honestly because much of our church cultures might come under close examination. And it is not just 'churchy' churches that might find themselves wanting; it might also be those large and 'successful' churches that unwittingly decide who can and who cannot have access to Jesus – all depending on whether or not they conform to the particular culture of that church and its people.

Jesus stops for those who see and know their need. Jesus' followers need to learn to do the same, constantly learning with humility to be open to examination and change. The Church should, after all, look something like Jesus. And Jesus rejected the screening nature of his followers and welcomed the 'outsider'.

Lord God, heal your Church so that your people might truly reflect your welcome and open embrace. Reshape us in company with each other and Jesus, that we might become agents of grace and not be obstacles to healing. Amen.

PERSONAL REFLECTION

What are the 'unclean' areas of my life, and how might the touch of Jesus bring healing? What might this look like in practice?

GROUP DISCUSSION

1. If the Church is truly the 'body' of Christ and, therefore, enfleshes the reality, presence and touch of Jesus today, who are the 'unclean' people who might be touched by us?

2. Where are the places of contamination in which the Church should be a healing presence or an agent of good news?

3. How is it possible for us to hear the Scriptures … and miss the point?

4. What might it mean for us to 'let go' of Jesus?

TEACHINGS

SUNDAY (LENT 3)

MARK 2:18–28   WHOSE SABBATH?

IT will be obvious by now that two themes dominate Mark's story: conflict (firstly, between Jesus and the authorities; secondly, between Jesus' perception of God's ways and that of his first followers) and surprise. From the beginning of the narrative, Jesus is causing a stir and making people ask serious questions about who he is and what he is up to. He keeps turning on its head the popular notion of what God is like and whose side God is on. For a people whose very identity has become tied up inextricably with the observance of a whole raft of rules, rituals and regulations, Jesus must have been extremely threatening. He takes what is sacred, subverts it, then questions what it was *for* in the first place. He constantly attempts to liberate God from the boxes of narrow expectations into which his people have forced him, and to liberate the people who have been imprisoned or disenfranchised by these systems of control.

The Sabbath lies at the very heart of what it means to be a Jew. As God rested on the Sabbath day, the seventh day of creation, so must his people bear witness to God's nature and activity by obediently resting from their own work. The question arises, however, as to what counts as work. As we have observed earlier, this is not an easy matter to question publicly because behind the question of Sabbath-observance hides a host of issues of social control, religious discipline and orthodoxy, and theological consistency. To subvert the Sabbath, therefore, is to stab at the heart of the faith and the society of people whose life is shaped by its observance in particular and regulated ways.

Jesus makes his mark by allowing his disciples to eat, drink and party while the orthodox are observing a fast. This looks to be deliberately provocative, almost inviting a challenge. It is possible, though, that the people who come to question why Jesus' friends are not fasting when everyone else is are simply curious. Surely, to disregard the rules so blatantly, Jesus must have some reason or rationale to support his behaviour? Jesus responds with three vivid but enigmatic images: a wedding, clothes and wine. This is typical of Jesus: use a picture and make the hearers do some work of their own in imagining what he means.

Fasting, Jesus suggests, is not a pointless ritual. Those who fast do so in order to look forward to that day when fasting will no longer be required – the day when the sovereign God of Israel is once again present among his people. Until then, the people will fast and remind themselves of who they are and what they are waiting for. Hence, for Jesus' friends to fast would suggest that they were still awaiting that day when God would come among them again ... when he was already there. When the bridegroom arrives at the place of marriage, the celebrations begin; the guests don't ignore him and continue waiting. If the presence of God is truly to be found enfleshed in Jesus of Nazareth, then his friends simply cannot be expected to fast. The point of their fasting has already been achieved. So, they must celebrate instead. The time will come when fasting will become valid once again, but that time is not now. Indeed, celebration itself witnesses to the identity of Jesus and makes a powerful claim in the eyes of the world. This is almost ironic: if people are fasting in order for the kingdom to come, why can't they see that it has?

Jesus then shifts the imagination further. If you tear a piece of clothing, you can repair it by sewing a patch over the hole. But if you are wise, you will stitch onto it a piece of older cloth and not a new piece. A new piece will shrink when washed, and the old cloth won't hold it; you will end up with an even worse problem than the one you began with. But sew on a piece of older, 'pre-shrunk' material and you will be fine. Is Jesus suggesting here that what he represents is not the radically new, a novel religion designed to supersede the old Judaism, but Judaism refreshed, thus allowing the faith to recover its original intention? Jesus clearly sees himself as the one who is fulfilling the original calling of Israel, not usurping or discarding it. This is important to understand even today, for the Scriptures do not make a good deal of sense unless we recognise this truth.

This point becomes even clearer when we come to the third image, wine-making. New wine has yet to complete its process of fermentation. Fermentation itself involves conflict and expansion of gases. Old wineskins may not be flexible enough to contain this fermentation, and the result will be a mess on the floor and a waste of good wine that could, in the right conditions, have matured. New wine doesn't go into 'new' wineskins either – despite what the English translations say; new wine goes into 'fresh' or 'refreshed' wineskins where it can continue its fermentation within flexible confines that allow its purpose to be served. Older wineskins would be soaked in water until their flexibility had been recovered, and these are the skins that would be most suitable for the new wine.

All this is richly evocative for followers of Jesus in any generation. Firstly, we recognise who Jesus is and celebrate the fact that our longings have been fulfilled: God is present among us in Jesus. Secondly, 'seeing' differently now, we don't simply reject the 'old religion' as defunct, but breathe new life into it by calling it back to its original purpose and vocation. Thirdly, God's people do not go in for novelty, arrogantly rejecting old forms in favour of the new; instead, we are to allow for refreshment, re-energising and reinvigorating of the old in order that it might become flexible enough once again to hold and allow the fermentation process to proceed in all its disturbing power.

And for us? Christians who reject the past and assume the right to set the 'novel' above the 'old' have clearly not understood Jesus or his message. Being called to rediscover the purpose of our rituals and ways of worshipping and living is not the same as being obliged to discard what we don't like. Jesus calls for recovery by refreshment.

Lord God, Jesus calls us to not lose sight of the purpose and end of our faith. He calls us to celebrate your presence among us in the world and thereby to be repairers of broken people and containers of maturing wine. Help us to be enriching and refreshing people, not stale or brittle in our life in your world for the sake of your world. Amen.

MONDAY (LENT 3)

MARK 4:1–20   SOWER AND SOILS

JESUS taught in such a way that the imagination of his hearers would be stimulated. It is simply a fact that most people in most cultures learn their view of the world by listening to stories. Stories put flesh and blood onto the bones of ideas and perspectives, teasing the mind and etching themselves into the memory of those who play with a story and its many dimensions. The most powerful form of storytelling now is probably to be found on a screen, with films, soap operas, plays and even documentaries providing a narrative by which something of the world can be learned, debated and understood. Stories are far more powerful for many people than the propagation of ideas on their own.

It is perhaps surprising that Jesus, having got into a boat on the lake, then takes as his visual aid something derived from land. He tells a simple story that would have been immediately understood by all those from this agricultural area, who would have been readily familiar with the distribution and fate of seeds and the farmers who sow them. It might be puzzling, then, that the disciples and (presumably) many others were not clear about the point of Jesus' parable. Isn't it blindingly obvious? Loads of people hear God's word, and most people reject it for all sorts of pathetic reasons, leaving only those blessed people ('us') who receive the word and let it grow within them. This means that those who claim to be friends of Jesus are those who understand the parable to be in their own favour.

However, all is not as it seems at first. Once again, those closest to Jesus don't grasp what he is saying and have to ask for further elucidation. Secondly, the same disciples appear not to have the courage to ask Jesus openly in such a way as to expose their ignorance. Perhaps their image of coherence matters more than a willingness to be open in their ignorance and humbly disregarding of how others see them. Perhaps this is the precursor of a church that feels it has to be clear and consistent about every matter of theology, ethics and doctrine for fear that failure on a single point would subvert its credibility in total. Where ignorance is seen as weakness, learning becomes impossible … and, in the case of the Church, it pushes Christians into an indefensible corner where reality does not easily intrude.

The reason Jesus is telling this parable is not in order to provide preachers with some way of measuring their effectiveness for generations to come. In fact, it is probable that such a question never entered his head. He tells this parable because he is (as we have already noted in these reflections on Mark and how he structured his gospel) now illustrating what he meant by his initial proclamation way back at the beginning of his public ministry: Israel's exile is over; God has returned to his Temple; God is present in Jesus; the kingdom is now among them and this is extremely good news; but, because this 'coming among them' has not happened according to the preconceived expectations of most people (especially the powerful and those whose theology was clearly tidier than

God's), most people do not or cannot or will not see it. Jesus' call to change the way they see and think about God, the world and themselves is too demanding and will eventually prove too threatening.

This points to the fact that Jesus is challenging again the way his own people understand God and his activity in Israel and the world. The kingdom of God has not exploded on the world in a blaze of military glory with the occupying Romans being ejected from the Promised Land and the people of Israel being vindicated in the eyes of the world. The messiah has not led his armies to victory, thus demonstrating the truth and validity of Israel's story – their self-understanding, identity, history and view of the future. No, the kingdom has crept up on them, silently infiltrating the present, getting sown into various soils and beginning to grow in surprising places where the vision is being glimpsed and followed by all the wrong people.

This, of course, begs one or two questions of 'the people of God' who have been eagerly awaiting the return of God and the coming of God's rule. Firstly, are God's people patient enough to wait for God's coming among them and for the kingdom to grow slowly? Or are they like many of today's Christians, insisting that God must work miracles *now*, and moving on swiftly if God seems not to answer specific demands (or 'prayers', as they are sometimes known) instantly? The story of the Bible is that God will not be rushed; his kairos will come when he is good and ready, and the job of his people is not to engineer his coming but to discern it. God's people, even today, need urgently to learn to wait for God, to learn patience as we try to see differently and to spot where God's kingdom is now present among us.

The second point emerges from a feature of the parable that is frequently overlooked: the sheer extravagance of the farmer's methodology. How do we see God? Is he passionately concerned that every seed should be sown in good soil and grow to bring the maximum fruit? Or is God just a bit too extravagant in the way he dispenses his seed? Shouldn't he be a bit more careful and a little less wasteful? But this is precisely what is so wonderfully vivid about the God and Father of Jesus: he is wasteful and outrageously extravagant in his generosity. He scatters his grace and love all over the place – even in places where it is unlikely to bear fruit. But God can't help himself; he throws the stuff all over the place and is happy to be thought too 'liberal'. It is not a huge leap to assume that he intends his people to behave in a similar way, not excluding people or limiting his grace, but being an accountant's nightmare ... and maybe even a Christian purist's nightmare.

Lord God, help your people to be less careful and less protective of your love and generosity. Where we are concerned always to count the cost and calculate the risk or return on our love, liberate us to be extravagant ... regardless of whether the seed we sow takes root and bears fruit. Amen.

TUESDAY (LENT 3)

MARK 4:21–5   LAMPS, BUCKETS AND BEDS

THE trouble with human imagination is that it can become overloaded. It is possible to become over-stimulated and want to stop the world for a time in order to catch up and think through what has been heard or seen or thought. Jesus, then, must have been a bit of a nightmare. He uses one image in his conversation, then immediately changes tack and alludes to a situation a million miles away from the first. Sowers and seeds are left behind while lamps, buckets and beds are conjured up in the minds of the audience.

Jesus' question is rhetorical; it doesn't need an answer. Why would anyone in their right mind switch on a light and then cover it up? It would be stupid, wouldn't it? It would be like putting a heavy-metal CD on the stereo and then turning the volume down to zero. Why would anyone do it? The whole point is that they wouldn't. And Jesus is addressing here a problem with God's people when they have good news and cover it up – an action that assumes the good news is for the people who know it and not for those who do not, as yet, know it. In other words, if God has illuminated your heart and mind with his grace and the recognition of his presence in the world, don't keep it to yourself … because it isn't for your personal entertainment or possession in the first place.

The interesting thing about a lamp is that it does not exist to be admired as a lamp. Yes, it is possible that we choose a particular lamp to stand in our lounge because we like its design and need its function. But a lamp is meant to illuminate – not itself, but all the stuff there is in the room. If a group of people in a house spent all evening staring at a lightbulb, admiring its shape and luminosity, we would think they were missing the point. They should be looking at what the light illuminates around them. In other words, the lamp helps them to see the world around them. Where the lamp is placed and how it shines will dictate how what is in the room is actually perceived. The shadows it throws are caused by the stuff that is placed in the room in the range of its beams. This might sound blindingly obvious, but it obviously isn't to some people … or Jesus wouldn't have used the image.

The people who are close to Jesus are catching a glimpse of what John in his gospel will call 'his glory'. They are seeing things happen because of Jesus and hearing teaching that is reshaping the lens behind their eyes through which they see God, the world and themselves. The world looks different when seen in the light of Jesus and his Father: legalism is challenged by grace, people cease to be religious or political pawns in games run by the powerbrokers; God is extravagant and wasteful with his grace and love, not tight-fisted and miserly in his bitterness. And, although the friends of Jesus are having to take all this in and allow their world-view to be radically challenged and reshaped, thus needing time and patience for the process of transformation to begin to take place, the time will come when they will simply be unable to keep it in. The way they see God, the world and themselves will so shape their behaviour, conversation, lifestyle and values that the whole world will see and know what they are about. This cannot be hidden for ever; the light will shine out and illuminate the world in new ways – values, relationships, behaviour – and offer a new perspective for all who witness it.

This process is common to all Christian disciples. Although the world we have grown up in tells us that there is a big divide between private and public, between fact and opinion, and that religion belongs firmly in the realm of mere private opinion, Christians cannot but see their experience and perception of God as illuminating the cosmos, shaping their life, casting shadows on a curious or hostile world. A Christian cannot keep his or her faith private and hidden … as if this fundamental element of life and motivation can be kept separate from anything that matters. Faith will out! The love and grace of God cannot be kept immersed under a veneer of respectability or niceness. The logic is clear: if you have been shaped by the grace of God, then you will not be able to stop yourself living a life with others that reflects that grace. A Christian will – or should – look something like Christ. And what does Jesus look like? Well, read this gospel and see! Then let his life and vision shine through your life and commitment.

But Jesus goes on to apply this further – and it comes in the form of a warning to those who claim to be God's people, seeing through God's eyes and blessed with the mark of his acceptance. Jesus is clear that, if we judge other people according to certain criteria, we should make sure that we ourselves are first judged against the same measure. This is what James keeps on about in his letter: it is no use using words of love and grace if you are ungracious and unloving to others. Don't be so arrogant as to claim to be 'Christian' (by believing the right things) if the evidence of your life tells the world you are not Christ-like. The reality of your faith will be seen by those who look through the lens of your words and actions and see what God and the world look like then.

This is at the same time both encouraging and sobering. We cannot take God and his favour for granted (be warned!), but neither should we be intimidated or impressed by those Christians whose behaviour tells a different story from their words and professed beliefs (be encouraged!). The truth will one day out, and we need not be worried in the meantime. God's light will shine in the darkness, and the darkness will never overcome it. In fact, as John observes in the prologue to his gospel, it already has ... in Jesus himself.

Lord God, who created light and darkness and, in Jesus, penetrated the darkness of the world with irrepressible light, illuminate our hearts and minds so that we may see the world and other people as you see them ... and live accordingly in this your world. Amen.

WEDNESDAY (LENT 3)

MARK 4:26–34   MORE SEEDS

SOME Christians seem obsessed with getting other Christians to sign up to a particular statement of faith. If you sign, you are 'kosher'; if you don't, you are somewhat suspect in your credentials. There seems to be almost a human compulsion to try to nail down every last jot and tittle of belief or to force complex ideas into straitjacketed forms of words. The problem some Christians find with creeds is that it is unclear whether the particular form of words is a bottom line (from which we explore) or a top line (beyond which we must not go).

It is interesting – though perhaps not surprising – that Jesus never *defines* the kingdom of God. Nowhere does he give us a three-line definition of what the kingdom of God is or where it is to be found. Rather, he keeps telling stories and offering suggestive pictures that seem to teem out of his fertile imagination. And these stories and pictures are more powerful than definitions precisely because they cannot be nailed down and used as weapons to threaten other people. Images and stories wheedle their way into the memory and tease the imagination of those who are interested enough to listen and think. They eat away at the edges of our vision and make us look differently at God, the world and ourselves. And, because they are images, they live and move and cannot be trapped even in the words used to frame them at first.

I can only assume that Jesus taught and talked in this way deliberately. He knew what he was doing when he avoided 'making points' and told stories instead. Presumably he also knew that images defy precision and ignite the imagination of the curious to the extent that the images might (like metaphors) get stretched into shapes not originally intended. Surely, when Jesus told his friends that they would have to become like little children if they were to enter God's kingdom, this is what he was getting at – for children are infinitely curious and won't have their curiosity squashed by unimaginative adults who have lost the ability to wonder and play.

Listening to Jesus using images and telling parables is a bit like lighting a theatre stage or shooting a scene on a film set. In one sense, you are looking at the same thing; but the different angles cast a different light, create an alternative shadow, suggest a slightly different perception of what is going on. He talks about the kingdom of God in a variety of ways that assume the rejection of a single dogma and open our minds to a playful variety of possibilities. To change the metaphor, we are not meant to examine the menu at the restaurant, discuss the cuisine with the chef, then leave without having eaten; rather, we are to get stuck into the different dishes and see what the cumulative taste is like.

So, Jesus returns in his language from lampstands and measuring-scales to an agricultural milieu. He tells of a farmer who has no idea how his seeds grow; but they grow anyway ... despite his ignorance. This insignificant little thing hides in the earth and grows into something big and useful before getting ripped up and made into something nutritious. When Jesus tells stories like this, he is consciously telling the story of his people, Israel. He is not going to make bald and bold statements that might be construed by suspicious hearers as politically seditious, so he uses images instead. But what could he possibly be trying to say that might be dangerous?

We have already seen in this gospel how Jesus claims that the presence of God is now back among the people of Israel, but that the very people who have been waiting and longing for the return of God's 'glory' seem unable to see the point. They expected the messiah to look rather different – more of a military commander, perhaps, leading the people to overthrow the Roman occupation, thus vindicating God's existence, presence and election of his people. So, Jesus doesn't quite fit the picture. All the evidence of their eyes tells them that the Romans are still in charge and looking fairly invincible; if God is here among them, he would probably show a bit more power and belligerence than this wandering preacher seems to do.

But Jesus is illustrating that the time will surely come when God's 'judgement' – his decisive presence recognised and his people's life measured against the character of the God to whom they have claimed to belong and whose life they should reflect – will come and be seen to have come. But it will come by surprise, not at all as they expected it. And this is politically sensitive at a time when the future of the people and their country is tied up with the fate of a massive hegemonic empire that doesn't like challenge. But the bit that is meant to shock the disciples when they first heard this is simply the fact that those who claim to be looking and longing for the judgement of God on the world are the same people who are consistently missing the point, looking in the wrong direction.

The disciples and those who watched them might be forgiven for not being terribly impressed with any claims to future glory. How could this ragbag of northern peasants be the powerhouse movement of God's renewing kingdom? How could anything glorious come out of such a small group of people who manage constantly to get the wrong end of the stick and later on will succeed in betraying, denying, misunderstanding and doubting their friend Jesus? But God's kingdom is like a tiny seed that grows into something large and useful, whose reach cannot be gainsaid. John Bell and Graham Maule of the Iona Community wrote a wonderful song called 'The Greatness of the Small' and in it described how it is that out of unlikely and tiny beginnings come powerful and transforming lives.

God's people are never simply to accept the evidence of their circumstances, but to see through the eyes of Jesus to the potential for his kingdom to grow. We might feel small, powerless and insignificant. But think how the world was changed by a tiny group of Palestinian peasants whose curiosity got teased by a wandering rabbi and whose tiny potential turned history upside down.

Lord God, you are the lover of small seeds, for out of them you can grow life-giving and nurturing plants. May we never despise the small, but see in it the potential for greatness, the power in the imperceptible to overthrow the judgements of the great. Amen.

THURSDAY (LENT 3)

MARK 9:38–50   THE COST OF FOLLOWING JESUS

JESUS is moving in dangerous territory. His reputation is growing, and the people are divided over his identity: is he from God, or not? The storm clouds of conflict are beginning to rumble in the distance, and theological differences are likely soon to give way to physical confrontation between Jesus and the powerful people who are threatened by him. But the question Mark is interested in here has not to do with the identity of Jesus, but rather with his disciples' awareness of the seriousness of this situation and potential confrontation. Soldiers go into battle knowing what sort of a war they are fighting; but these disciples, squabbling among themselves about status and kudos, run the risk of finding themselves in a place of conflict unprepared for what might happen to them. If they are ignorant or unprepared, the chances are that they will fall at the first sound of gunfire.

Scan the rows of colour magazines on any news-stand and it will become blindingly obvious that the world we live in today sees personal fulfilment as the right and ultimate goal of humanity. How this sense of fulfilment is to be reckoned can usually be reduced to physical attractiveness, sexual satisfaction, material well-being and 'successful' living. Christians are not exempt from drinking from the pool in which we inevitably also swim. Christian bookshops are full of books about successful living, victorious faith, God's desire for Christians to be wealthy (as a sign of God's favour) and decidedly partial theologies of personal 'salvation'. Being a Christian, however, is not a romantic holiday for those who find Jesus attractive. Discipleship is about following the Jesus who gets nailed to a cross and bids his friends join him. Discipleship involves cost, fulfilment through loss not profit, through suffering not 'health and beauty'.

Although the cultures in which discipleship has to be exercised today differ considerably from that of first-century Palestine, the temptation to miss the point remains the same. John and his colleagues might be enjoying the radical subversion of Jesus' actions and teaching, but not everybody is happy with these developments. Soon, the knives will come out and it will then be too late for the disciples to think through what following Jesus might entail. So, Jesus warns them to 'get real', to face the truth about themselves and the journey they are on. They must choose for themselves whether or not Jesus is messiah; if he is, they will find it hard to live consistently with their judgement when the heat is on and their own lives are at stake. In other words, Jesus is telling them to wake up to the impending conflict and face the cost of being a follower of the messiah.

It is important to note that Jesus does not imply that his friends should give up things that are slightly seductive; he cites good and 'essential' things in life such as hands, feet and eyes. He is exaggerating to make a point: don't let anything get in the way of your discipleship; deny yourself anything that will distract you from being proclaimers of the good news of God's kingdom come among them in Jesus; wake up to the fact that the situation is serious and this is not a jolly holiday to make you feel better about yourselves, more 'personally fulfilled'.

But there is another warning in here that rings bells for contemporary Christians as it has for God's people throughout the ages. It has to do with ownership of the gospel and the Church. While the disciples are busy squabbling and trying to work out what is going on in and through Jesus, other people are proclaiming the good news and setting people free from the things that bind and enslave them. John (no doubt on behalf of the others) protests to Jesus that this privilege belongs to those who are the 'inner circle' of Jesus' followers. But the embarrassing truth that has to be faced by the 'inner circle' is that neither the gospel nor the Church belongs to them. The disciples (prototype Church) are to be caught up in the proclamation by word and deed of the good news, but they do not possess or claim it. It is for Jesus to allow who should do and say what in his name; it is not the responsibility of his disciples to decide whom Jesus should call to ministry in his name.

This hammers home the difficult notion (for some of us in the Church) that the mission of the Church in the world is God's mission. And it is for God to choose who should be engaged in that mission. If Christians (those who consider themselves to be decidedly 'in') are too busy squabbling and fighting over this matter and that ethical issue, then others will do the mission of God instead. What is clear, however, is that the mission of God to heal the world will not be thwarted by narrow-minded ego-merchants who are content to be distracted by all sorts of noble matters (hands, feet and eyes) while the world continues to bleed.

This is uncomfortable stuff for serious Christian disciples. Just as Jerusalem would fall at the hands of the rampaging Roman Empire and its Temple be destroyed in the process, so will God's people share that fate if they do not get their priorities right. Preservation of power, control or even the right to decide who is 'in' and who is 'out' are not to preoccupy those who follow Jesus; salt exists not for its own sake but for the sake of that which it is there to preserve.

The call to discipleship has never changed. Those who follow Jesus have to face reality and address the potential cost. If the first disciples struggled to recognise the seriousness of the choices before them, there is little to indicate that the Church of our day has made a great deal of progress. While churches fight and divide over matters such as sexuality, millions die from poverty, hunger and AIDS. If the Church doesn't get its calling right, who else might Jesus be calling to do his work … despite the Church?

Lord God, set your people free to hear afresh the call to follow Jesus. Grant us the courage to face the cost of discipleship. Open our eyes to the needs of your world, our ears to the cries of your people, our hearts to the passion of God for his world. Amen.

FRIDAY (LENT 3)

MARK 10:1–16   DIVORCE AND CHILDREN

IT is not always either wise or tactful to say exactly what you mean. The first rule of communication is this: it is not what you say that matters, but what people *hear* you say. So, sometimes it is wise to be cautious in how words are used, or else the consequences of misunderstanding or misrepresentation might be serious.

This is the position Jesus finds himself in when the Pharisees try again to trap him into saying something they can manipulate against him. The battle of wits never seems to let up. So, when Jesus is asked a seemingly straightforward question about divorce, he responds in a way that defies contradiction by his opponents (he quotes Moses and the creation ordinances in Genesis), but opens up the issue rather than closes it down. Two things need to be noted if this is to become clear: firstly, Jesus is in the Judaean desert where John the Baptiser has just fallen foul of Herod's relationship games (he has just married his brother's wife), so he has to be careful with his words; secondly, divorce was open to abuse by the powerful (men) as a means of convenience, thus dehumanising the vulnerable women and children involved.

In this encounter with the Pharisees, Jesus publicly states that marriage is more than a legal contract and involves the uniting of two people in a new 'body'. To end this is not a trivial matter, and the baseline of any judgement here must begin with God's ideal purpose for human relationships. Exceptions might be possible – desirable even – but his concern here is simply to establish the bottom line. In private with his friends, however, he rams home the seriousness of the matter.

Now, this encounter and Jesus' response to it open up questions of God's desire for Israel and its modelling of good and godly relationships for the sake of the watching and wondering world. The 'hard-heartedness' that prevented Israel from fulfilling God's call to it from the beginning led the utterly realistic Moses to be permissive about divorce in some circumstances where the ideal is not possible. And Jesus does not deny this in his response, but still wants to stress the line from which permissive generosity must begin. But why?

Jesus is at pains throughout the gospel to demonstrate God's bias towards the vulnerable and the excluded. Those who have been told (usually by religious men) that they are of no account or are too unclean for God find in Jesus' embrace a welcome that is shocking. Those who have been abused or marginalised discover from the words, actions and priorities of Jesus that God is on their side. Those who have no name and no place in the community of God's people find themselves restored and given a new dignity. Those who were deemed 'blind' by the religious powermongers hear themselves pronounced 'seeing' by Jesus ... because they get the point of who he is and what he is about.

It is no surprise, then, that following the statement about divorce Jesus gets angry again. (Whatever happened to 'Gentle Jesus, meek and mild'?) His friends are the ones who should 'see' clearly what he is about; but they are also the ones who try to keep the vulnerable away from Jesus. People start bringing their children to be touched by Jesus, and the disciples try to keep them away. They just don't make the connections between the theology and the practice! No doubt his friends thought that Jesus had more important things to do than mess around with children, who, after all, are not going to be much use to him in his ministry and mission.

But Jesus will not be fobbed off by 'protectors' who want to guard him from intrusion by those who can't contribute to the cause. He sees that people are not to be measured by their usefulness or by their present 'value'. So, just as he is concerned in his comments about divorce to protect those (women) who can be easily disposed of for the convenience of a man, so here he wants to protect the value and status of those who might be seen as just getting in the way. Children, he demonstrates, are closer to the kingdom of God (the presence and affection of Jesus) than those adults whose experience and thought-patterns have led them to a utilitarian view of both God and other people. Marriage partners are not to be treated as disposable conveniences; children have as much access to the heart of God as do adults, even though children contribute little to the 'balance sheet' of religious or commercial life.

But this is not all. Jesus is very strong in his statement about children and the kingdom of God: it belongs to them … and adults had better work out how to be like the children if they are serious about entering God's kingdom/presence. But what does he mean? Many people assume that he (naïvely) thought of children as being sweet and innocent.

But two things that characterise children are their infinite curiosity and their capacity for play. Adults have both of these drummed out of them as they grow up and adapt to society's pressures and expectations. But children cannot be stopped from asking 'why' at inappropriate moments and are damaged if they are not given the space, encouragement and permission to play imaginatively.

Jesus seems to be saying that the kingdom of God is characterised by the presence of the vulnerable, who keep asking questions and know how to wonder, and who cannot be stopped from playing and using their imagination.

Now, where does this leave us and our churches? Are we characterised by our openness to the vulnerable or our adherence to religious rules? Does the local community see a church that knows how to play and celebrate or one that squashes imagination into dogmatic boxes and defies anyone to trespass outside of them? Do we belong to (and create) a church in which adults are open to learn from children, even if the results are sometimes messy?

Jesus refused to be protected by his followers, embraced the children and hugged them. There is no evidence to suggest that he has changed his priorities even if, sometimes, the Church appears to suggest otherwise.

Lord God, thank you that Jesus was not susceptible to being protected. Thank you that he exposes our limited vision and hard-hearted attitudes. Help us to make the space for vulnerable and abused people to find the embrace of Jesus. And help us to see in the face of our children the nature and complexion of your kingdom. Amen.

SATURDAY (LENT 3)

MARK 12:1–12   TENANTS WHO FORGET

SOME stories don't need any further explanation or commentary; they speak for themselves. One of the things that strikes a reader of the gospels is how Jesus uses stories to make the hearers engage imaginatively and not just intellectually with his world-view. You can take or leave a propositional statement, but a story draws you in and makes you find your place within it. And this is how parables work. In some cases, Jesus has to explain himself later; but the story he tells here speaks loudly and clearly for itself.

Countries, societies, even businesses claim for themselves a symbol or icon that is intended to say something about who they are and what they are about. The old Soviet Union used the hammer and sickle to claim that this was a country based on the power of working people in agriculture and industry – the dictatorship of the proletariat, as it was known in Marxist terms. The Union Jack combines the crosses of three kingdoms, thus speaking of a history born self-consciously in Christian mission and united centuries ago under a single throne. The Israel of Jesus' time had grown to recognise itself in terms of a vineyard, planted by God himself and destined to bring forth harvests of full and nourishing grapes. But, as with the Soviet icons and the elements of the Union Jack, symbols are always open to different interpretations and the telling of competing stories.

The Old Testament prophet, Isaiah, described Israel as a vineyard that had stopped producing its fruit, thus making it susceptible to being ripped up by the owner and destroyed. If Israel did not recover its fundamental calling (to be God's people for the sake of the world, thus bearing fruit for the nurturing and savouring of the world), its fate was not going to be a pleasant one. The rest of Isaiah fleshes out this warning and describes vividly the bitter experiences of those who endured this 'ripping up' in exile and powerlessness.

So, when Jesus tells the religious people of his day a story about a vineyard, everyone makes an immediate association: he is talking about us and he is not being very complimentary. In fact, he appears to be rewriting the story we thought we had grasped, and now he is turning it against us. Choosing to speak of a vineyard was asking for trouble.

The story behind the parable reads something like this. God planted his people for the benefit of his world. However, they forgot the purpose and object of their calling and arrogated to themselves as a possession that which God had given them. God will not be taken for granted – especially by his own people – and sends people to call the people back to their original vocation. Their warnings and encouragements are not well received, and these faithful messengers find themselves abused and rejected by those who do not want their lives, priorities or values disturbed. But God does not just give a clear warning once; he repeatedly sends his prophets to speak truth into their situation, offering many opportunities for the people to hear and respond. But every opportunity is wasted, and in the end God sends his own flesh and blood – which in these terms is like sending himself. The tragedy is that even his son is rejected, abused and destroyed.

What is remarkable, however, is that the story doesn't end there. Human violence and destruction will not and cannot have the final word. God is not defeated, even by the worst that human beings can do to his creation or himself. And here is the most appalling warning of all: if Israel will not recover its calling, God will take away from it the privilege of being a specially chosen people and confer it on some other people.

This idea in itself is fundamentally anathema to the people of Jesus' time. The threat of ceasing to be God's people is so outrageous as to be at best unthinkable and at worst blasphemous. In fact, to embrace such a notion as this would mean such a radical and daring change of mindset and an openness to the possibility that the received and accepted theological ideas about God, the world and this people would have to be reshaped and reinterpreted. This was surely asking too much.

Well, the story reflects the unfolding tragedy of Jesus himself and this people – his people – who cannot bear to hear that God doesn't see things as they have grown to do. The prophets have gone unheeded, and even the resulting exile has not done the job of converting the people's minds to God's way of seeing and being. So, the time is now coming when even God's own flesh and blood will be rejected. And Mark sees this story moving the narrative on towards the violent and appalling climax of Calvary. Jesus' words and actions, demonstrating the presence of God among them, have gone unheeded by the very people who have longed and prayed for generations that God's presence would return. The irony is bitter.

It is clear that the religious authorities recognised the target of the story but couldn't entertain the possibility that it might be true. It didn't fit their shape, so they rejected it angrily and began to look for ways of getting rid of the man telling such stories. The irony is bitter – but they couldn't see the parallels, being blinded to the light of God's liberating and healing presence among them.

Before being too critical of these stubborn people, we might need to ask ourselves how willing we might be to rethink our theology and change our lives accordingly. It is easy to ask other people to 'repent' while ignoring the need for us to be open to the same invitation or challenge. Again, we might need to recognise that it is often those closest to the 'centre' of religious (even Christian) faith who are in most danger of missing the point. It is repeatedly the case in Mark's gospel that those closest to Jesus, those most passionate for the Scriptures and those most keen on being faithful to God's call are the ones who are blind … while those who appear to be blind actually see most clearly.

If the point of Jesus' story was obvious to those who heard him and took it personally, then the challenge of that last paragraph is for Christian readers of the gospel to examine first their own readiness to be 'transformed by the renewing of their mind' (Romans 12:2), subjecting their own theological understanding of God, the world and themselves to scrutiny and criticism.

Lord God, give us the grace to hear your word to us so that we will see clearly and not miss your presence among us. Deliver us from the blindness that prevents us from seeing the face of Jesus and replaces it with something more attractive to our preferred priorities. Amen.

PERSONAL REFLECTION

In what sense is my faith personal but not private?

In what sense does my faith encourage child-like curiosity about God, the world and people?

GROUP DISCUSSION

1. How are we to distinguish between 'novelty' and 'fresh expression' in the life and witness of the Church? How can we know how to discern when 'refreshment' rather than 'replacement' is needed in the life and worship of the Church?

2. Are we really open to being surprised by the Jesus who subverts our expectations and preferences?

3. How might the Church express the outrageous, extravagant generosity of God as exemplified by the farmer in the parable of the sower?

4. How can we learn to tease the curiosity of people about God and Jesus rather than tell them what to believe and how to behave?

5. Does God need to be protected or defended by Christians against 'unwelcome' intrusions?

HAPPENINGS

SUNDAY (LENT 4)

MARK 4:35–41   CALMING THE STORM

PEOPLE who have grown up by or near the sea find it very difficult to live in an inland urban place. I grew up in Liverpool and still miss the sound of seagulls, the smell of the brine on the wind and the fresh air that blows in off the ocean. For me, the sea was a mysterious place that beckoned the traveller over the horizon towards all sorts of unknown experiences and places. The sea spoke of openness, beauty and possibility. However, when I was 21, I endured the most horrendous Channel crossing and became frighteningly aware of the power of the deep. When the sea is wild, it symbolises all that is most terrifying about life and the world, evoking a sense of pitiful smallness and powerlessness in anyone subject to its ferocity. (And that is why the vision of John in Revelation 21 reveals that there is no sea in the new earth – it symbolises everything destructive and turbulent about the world.)

It is no wonder, then, that the wild sea represented for Jesus' friends and contemporaries all that was wrong and frightening about the world. The sudden furious winds that would get whipped up around Galilee were still enough to terrify even those men who had lived and worked on the sea all their lives. And so this episode represents for Mark a parallel to the experience of Israel, of Jesus and of his friends as they weave their own ways through history. Everything is turbulent, and it will appear as if violence and destruction (especially at the hands of the mighty Roman Empire) rule over life itself; but all of this is to be transformed by the presence of God in the world.

For Israel at the time of Jesus, the questions are unresolved: how long will the humiliation of our occupation and oppression continue? Who will be the one to liberate us from this suffering and welcome the glory/presence of God among us again? Through whom will our peace come, relieving us of this turbulence? Of course, the answer is in front of their very eyes; but they don't recognise it.

For the disciples of Jesus, now beginning to see and hear the good news of God's kingdom come in Jesus himself, life is going to get extraordinarily tougher. The opposition to Jesus (and, by association, to them also) is going to grow, and the dream of a bright future is going to dissolve into a night time of horror and desolation. Having caught a glimpse of the presence of God among them in the person and ministry of Jesus, he is to be violently torn away from them and his whole project thrown into apparent catastrophe. Their world will be turned upside down, threatened and beaten to a pulp, leaving them distraught on a turbulent 'sea' over which they have no control. Life for these people is not going to get easier.

But they will discover that God is not persuaded by the turbulence of the world that he is a victim of it. Rather, he experiences the suffering of the world and the fears of its people along with them, but is not intimidated by their power. Jesus sleeps through the violent storm and has to be woken by those who feel their existence to be threatened by forces beyond their control. Jesus calms the storm and leaves his friends musing on the identity of their friend and leader.

It is in the nature of things that the disciples probably did not grasp the full significance of this experience until they came (like Mark) to reflect on it in the light of Gethsemane and Calvary and the road to Emmaus. The enacted parable would only make sense as such once events had gone further and the horrors had been endured. But Mark presents us with this episode early on in his account, offering a memory point for later when we hear the faint echo of it in the following events of the gospel narrative.

Apart from its place in the developing story, this event also raises questions for us today. Is Jesus indifferent to the suffering of his people? Does he simply sleep when the world around us is in turmoil and our faith is profoundly challenged by powers beyond our control? Does he really leave us alone to get on with it while he nods off, unaffected by the things that intimidate us? The answers to this might be surprising.

This gospel demonstrates that Jesus was anything other than indifferent to the fate of his friends. Indeed, he kept warning them about what lay ahead, even recognising that they would not fully understand his meaning until they had gone through the terrible experiences of his torture, death and resurrection. He sleeps in the boat not in ignorance of what is happening outside, but despite it. The world will always be turbulent and unpredictable, but Jesus and his people learn that the evidence of their eyes does not tell the whole story. Jesus' friends are not exempted from all that the world can throw at them. Being a follower of Jesus does not qualify anyone for an easy life somehow abstracted from the world's powers and absurdities.

But the transforming nature of the experience lies in our discovery of the presence of God in Jesus among us and with us. In other words, we might be transformed within the circumstances to see through the troubles to the calmer place.

But the truth is also that the disciples are not spared any future similar experience. This would not be the last time their lives would be in danger from powers beyond their control. They remain at sea even when Jesus has calmed it for the time being.

Christians (especially in their theology of healing) must come to terms with their mortality before they begin to think about resurrection. We must face our place in a contingent world, not expecting God to preserve us at all costs from suffering, illness, abuse or death. But we will discover in the midst of these that God is present, though sometimes hidden for a while. And, if the calmness is restored once, it does not mean that no further trouble will befall us. We are meant to discover what the presence of God in the world means, not that the presence of God takes us out of the world.

Lord God, be present with us and those whom we love when life becomes disturbed and dangerous. Preserve us from the urge to escape the world and empower us to trust you in both the turbulence and the calm. Amen.

MONDAY (LENT 4)

MARK 6:1–13   SENT OFF

THERE was a time when every church seemed to
have what was called a 'Family Service'. This was
intended to provide a form of worship service that
was accessible to all ages – the whole family. However,
many churches have now dropped the name, even if
they have continued to pursue a form of service that
is accessible to people of all ages and stages of life.
One reason the name has been dropped is that the
word 'family' is ambiguous: does it refer to the church
family or the nuclear family? If it refers to the nuclear
family, it has become an embarrassment because there
are now so many different manifestations of 'family'.
And where does it put single people or those whose
family has been torn apart by loss, death, divorce or
desertion? For many churches, the word 'family' has
become problematic.

Jesus didn't get near anything like a Family
Service, but he did experience much of the frustration
that comes with belonging to a family – any family of
any shape or size. When he had something serious to
say, his family didn't take him seriously. After all, they
all knew him and had grown up with him. They knew
the things that they liked about him and the things that
irritated them. So, when he taught from the Scriptures
in the synagogue on the Sabbath, they missed the

point he was trying to make because they couldn't get beyond the mental block that this was 'their' Jesus. The best way to imagine this is to ask how you would respond if your older brother one day announced he was a prophet in whom the longed-for presence of God was now to be found.

It might also come as a bit of a surprise that even Jesus can be surprised. It is easy to run away with the idea that Jesus knew everything and could be surprised by nothing. But even he was taken by surprise by the inability or unwillingness of his own family and neighbours to think about what he was saying. Bemused by their stubbornness, he leaves the town and wanders round the surrounding villages trying to see if his message gets a better hearing there.

There are hints here of a problem that besets all those who claim a familiarity with Jesus in any form, and it is this: it is possible to be so close to Jesus that we miss the point of what he is saying and what he is about. If he does not conform to what he expect him to say or do, we just assume that he couldn't possibly have meant what he appears to be saying. We shape him in our own image and shape what he says to suit the preconceived form we have already decided (on other grounds) that he must mean. Hence we lose the ability to be challenged by him because we are only able to hear what we think he ought to be saying. But, as this passage suggests, this is not a new experience for Jesus. Rejection was not the sole prerogative of his enemies.

It is perhaps not so surprising, then, that immediately following this experience Jesus sends out his twelve closest friends to start doing 'kingdom stuff' for themselves. Telling them about the kingdom and letting them witness its characteristics (healing, deliverance and proclamation) is not enough. They could easily assume that only Jesus could do these things; but Jesus wants them to see that if the kingdom has come in the person of Jesus, then the kingdom can be seen in the world mediated through his friends. In other words, those who proclaim the good news, heal and deliver in the name of Jesus will also see that the kingdom is here, brought into the world by Jesus himself.

The point of it all was that ordinary people would see that the presence (kingdom) of God had indeed broken in and that the evidence was there to be seen and experienced. The twelve would take the message out in many different directions, and people would have to respond in some way or other to what they heard and witnessed. Some would welcome the 'good news', but others would shut it out – for a host of reasons, including an unwillingness to have their life and world-view disturbed. The mission was urgent, and the twelve were not to waste their time on those who were stubbornly resistant but were to take the news to as many people as possible.

However, there is also a symbolism here that speaks as loudly in Mark's mind as the actions themselves. Israel's history is marked by the Twelve Tribes who, despite their calling to be a blessing to the world, have by now all but disappeared. When Jesus sends out twelve men, he is making a vivid statement: this is Israel recreated and renewed, being sent out into the world to fulfil what had been Israel's original calling anyway – to be a blessing to the world. After years of judgement, absence and exile, now God was renewing his people and calling them to demonstrate the presence of God in the world calling his people to rethink (repent) their understanding of God and their history.

There is a strong hint here of the later calling of the Church. After the traumatic experiences of crucifixion and resurrection, followed in due course by the Roman destruction of Jerusalem and the Temple in AD 70, Christians would be dispersed throughout the world. They would be persecuted, rejected and resisted, but some people would hear and see and believe. Their reshaped minds, fired by their experience of the presence of God in Jesus, devastated by crucifixion and shocked by resurrection, led them to proclaim in word and deed their conviction that Israel had been renewed and its calling revalidated. This faith was not a private matter, but very public. It would invite opposition and create serious enemies. But people would also be blessed by their discovery that God is on their side, inviting them to be his renewed people.

That is still the calling of Christians today.

Lord God, give to your people today the curiosity, courage and faith to go out in your name to bring your good news to our family, friends and neighbours. May we have the confidence in you to respond to your call, even if it means being sent where we would rather not go. Amen.

TUESDAY (LENT 4)

MARK 6:30–44   FEEDING THE 5,000

THE danger of isolating a text in a particular book of the Bible is that we make it say what we want it to say, or that we miss the contextual information and hidden signs that make it understandable. Hence, a reading of the feeding by Jesus of 5,000 people easily becomes a miracle intended to convince observers of his great supernatural powers. But such a reading is simplistic and misses the richness contained in Mark's relating of the event in the course of his cleverly woven narrative. The feeding of the 5,000 is many-layered and intended to say something about the identity and calling of Jesus, the responsibility of his followers and just how God's presence brings order out of chaos … as in creation itself.

The context is this. The question of who Jesus is has been asked implicitly and explicitly from the outset of the gospel. Jesus has sent out his chosen twelve 'apostles' (literally the 'sent ones') to start enfleshing in the world what Jesus has enfleshed for them. They are not simply to follow Jesus around enjoying the amazing things he does and says; they have to start doing them for themselves in his name, according to his ways and consistent with his character and priorities. But this would be a little easier if the process wasn't rudely interrupted by the speculations of Herod about the identity (and, therefore, threat) of Jesus and by his brutal treatment of John the Baptiser. For the disciples, this is more than a little confusing: Jesus brings healing to people but evokes opposition from the very people whose lives revolve entirely around an expectation and hope of God's return. John has paved the way for Jesus, opening the minds and hearts of the people to the possibility of God's return among them now. And his reward? He is executed in brutal fashion by the very king who is supposed to be the shepherd of God's people in a dangerous world. And this puts the disciples in a difficult position because they might easily prove to be Herod's next prison and party guests.

So, the disciples come back to Jesus after their first excursion in his name, and he thinks they need a bit of a break. New ministry is demanding and exhausting, and space for reflection and rest is vital. They jump in the boat, but are spotted and the crowds second-guess their intended destination. When the boat comes in to land, the crowds are already there waiting for Jesus and his friends.

When it comes to welcoming intrusions into Jesus' space, the track record of Jesus' friends in this gospel is not exactly good. Despite being close to Jesus and witnessing his embrace for the vulnerable and excluded, they try to protect Jesus. So, we can only guess at their reaction when they came round the headland and saw the crowds waiting for them. Were they tempted to sail on to somewhere else? All we know is that, when Jesus got out of the boat and saw the crowds, he did not run away or get back in the boat and sail away. Rather, he saw the people as they truly were: like sheep without a shepherd. This image needs a little explanation.

The kings of Israel were viewed in terms of shepherding throughout the Old Testament. The shepherd was supposed to guard and guide the sheep, protecting them with his own life. The shepherd consciously did not own the sheep, but cared for them on behalf of the owner, representing the owner in his behaviour and care. The shepherd was not a hired worker, simply paid to do a piece of work without any deeper responsibility; he was engaged in body, soul and mind in the exercise of this responsibility. Herod was supposed to fulfil this calling for the sake of his oppressed people. But Herod was compromising his position all over the place, both in his personal behaviour and in his public collusion with the seductive powers. He was, in fact, a bad shepherd, neglecting his flock and letting them go where they will, whatever the danger. This shepherd cared about himself and his own interests above those of his people. Herod fed himself while his sheep starved for want of leadership. And Jesus saw this all too clearly.

So, Jesus steps into the role of the good shepherd and feeds the sheep with his teaching about God, the world and people. The disciples then revert to type and suggest (probably because of their own hunger, hinted at in verse 31) that Jesus send the people away to get food for themselves. But Jesus embarrasses them again by asking them to take responsibility for those about whom they appear to care little. The friends of Jesus are invited to make a material reality of the spiritual sustenance Jesus has been giving to the sheep without a shepherd, the people without a leader. In one sense, Jesus is refusing to allow the separation of the spiritual from the material. He will not simply indulge his friends by doing what they should be doing.

One immediate echo here with our own experience resounds in our exercise of prayer. No Christian should ever hear himself or herself praying for God to do something about a situation (any situation) without then seeking ways to answer the prayer by personal action. It would appear that, if we ask God to feed the hungry people in our communities, he might well tell us to do it for him. The worrying thing is that the seriousness of our spirituality will be measured by the extent to which we 'do' what we want or expect God to do on our behalf.

Clearly, there are echoes here of the feeble, broken 'bread' of Jesus' tortured and crucified body, weak and destroyed, yet exploding out into the world bringing nurture and healing to the hungry and exhausted. The sharing of limited resources by limited people with limited vision transforms the experience of ordinary people simply because it is done in obedience to Jesus' invitation and command. The friends of Jesus are called simply to join their resources, do a bit of organisation of people, then give away what Jesus has taken, broken, blessed and handed to his sceptical friends.

The miracle here is less to do with large numbers of people being fed; after all, they would no doubt be hungry again tomorrow, and the implication of the text is that they could have gone away and found food for themselves anyway. The miracle is rather more to do with the breaking-in of God's kingdom, fulfilling in Jesus the calling of Israel and its leaders/shepherds, and drawing ordinary, sceptical people into using their gifts to nurture and feed others. The spiritual is measured in material terms; the material becomes the stuff of spiritual priority.

Lord God, open our eyes that we might see the people of our communities and our world as Jesus sees them. Move us also to use our gifts and resources in feeding your people, both materially and spiritually. Amen.

WEDNESDAY (LENT 4)

MARK 6:45–56   WALKING ON WATER

MARK almost falls over himself as he drives his narrative forward, urging those with 'the eyes to see' to get the point about Jesus. We are constantly faced with questions about the true nature and identity of Jesus and the response of his friends and enemies to what they observe him doing and saying. Sometimes we are made to look at the religious authorities and recognise their inability or unwillingness to engage with the powerful and radical things Jesus is both saying and demonstrating about God. At other times, however, we are made to look at the close friends of Jesus and their stuttering glimpses and recognitions of who Jesus is, spotting perhaps in them some of the limitations and messiness we see in ourselves and our own faltering attempts to follow Jesus.

Here, in the episode on the lake, we are confronted by Jesus and his friends. We read that the disciples didn't understand what they had been part of in the feeding of the 5,000 'because their hearts were hardened'. It was going to be a long time before they would see the significance of what they had witnessed – and Jesus never seems to be in the business of getting people to run before they can walk. But the underlying observation here is that, by not understanding what it is they are seeing, they continue to miss the point about exactly who Jesus is. They see him walking on the water and are terrified – but so they should be if they don't grasp what it means for Jesus to be the presence of God among them, bringing into focus the new relationship between humanity and God's created world.

This should be encouraging and comforting for all those who want to follow Jesus. Jesus chose ordinary people and allowed them the space and time to learn and grow and rethink God, the world and themselves. He did not damn them for their ignorance and inconsistency. He did not suspect their motives when they failed to get the point. He was unsurprised by their limitations and unshocked by their contradictions. For Jesus, there was no 'counsel of perfection' leading him to stand in judgement on the fallibilities or theological blindness of his friends. It was enough that they were on a journey with him, and things would work out in their own good time.

But the event is also intended by Mark to raise again the question that was so baffling for the disciples: who is this Jesus, and where does he fit into the theological constructs by which we see and understand life, history and the world we know?

Jesus is seen here as the archetype of true humanity. Jesus is the long-awaited messiah, the one in whom God is present and through whom he will lead his people to freedom. But, as we have seen repeatedly, he isn't 'doing messiah' as the people thought their script stated he should. He didn't seem to be shaped like the one they were expecting. So, either he was an impostor (yet another pretender to Israel's throne) or their expectations were wrong and needed some reshaping. Mark is clear that the latter is the case and that his readers/hearers must keep facing the tough question about the true identity of Jesus. Is he the one in whom the glory of God has returned to his people? Is he the one who will liberate his people and end their exile? And, if he is, then what does this say about God's intentions for his people in the world? And, furthermore, what does it suggest 'liberation' might look like (especially if it does not involve the eviction of the Roman imperial powers from the land)?

Well, Jesus walks on the lake while his friends battle against the wind on the same lake. Already we have seen Jesus calm a storm and feed thousands of people. Now he appears once again to exercise dominion over the created order, bringing order out of chaos and implicitly playing the role of the Creator himself. The messiah, Israel's true and returning king, will exercise sovereignty over the world, and this is demonstrated here in Jesus' sovereignty over food and water. The claim stands by itself, to be recognised by those who can be bothered to look and to think about it. This is a miracle designed not to convince people of Jesus' divinity (how would it prove that, after all?) but to enflesh the reality that in Jesus God's rule brings together both the divine presence and human vocation. Mark includes it here to make us work it out (although he doesn't even hint at where Jesus was heading and why walking on water to get there was absolutely necessary!).

But that is not the end of the matter either. The words that Jesus says to the startled disciples who are terrified by the 'ghost' are deeply significant – not just of who Jesus is, but also of how Jesus is with his fickle and fragile followers. 'It's me! Don't be afraid.' The implication is that fear is dispelled when we recognise the presence of Jesus with us in surprising places. He doesn't tell his friends to get a grip or grow up or remember their theology. He doesn't castigate them for their hardness of heart or troublesome faith. He simply identifies himself as the one who is with them and tells them not to fear. This will be repeated many times on the lips of Jesus as he invites bewildered people to surrender their fear and to trust him.

For frail and inconsistent followers of Jesus (which means all of us), this is a great relief and encouragement. Jesus is not surprised by our ignorance or fear and doesn't damn us for either. Instead, he beckons us to recognise him as messiah, the one who brings the presence and the glory of God into the most frightening and difficult of places and urges us to lose our fear – not because our circumstances have necessarily changed, but simply because he is there in them with us.

Lord God, help us to recognise your presence in the hard and frightening places of our lives. Enable us to be people who lead others to lose their fear by encountering you in the turbulent waters of our world. Amen.

THURSDAY (LENT 4)

MARK 8:31–9:1   PREDICTIONS

YOU really can't help feeling sorry for the disciples of Jesus. They are just getting their minds round what they have been seeing and hearing from Jesus – and then he seems to change tack again. They are just beginning to comprehend that Jesus might be the messiah, the one sent by God to deliver the people and restore the Temple, when Jesus tells them that he is going to be killed. But an idea such as this doesn't fit into their script. The whole point about the messiah was that he would be the one to deliver Israel and vindicate the claims of Israel to be God's people. They would recognise the messiah when his leadership led to the eviction of the Roman overlords and the restoration of the Temple to its former glory and true purpose.

So, when Jesus told them he was going to be killed, this didn't make any sense. Peter's response was to scold Jesus for talking nonsense. Within his mindset, there wasn't a slot for 'dead messiah'; the two words couldn't be put together like that. So Peter was not being difficult when he remonstrated with Jesus about his statement; he was simply being consistent with his received notion of what a messiah should be and do.

It is important at this point to recognise what has immediately preceded this passage (which will be explored more fully in a later section of this book).

Mark writes that Peter has finally been put on the spot and invited to articulate his conclusions about the true identity of Jesus. He declares that Jesus is the messiah. Well, that is fine except that his understanding of what 'messiah' is (or should be) is what today might be termed 'unreconstructed'. So, when Jesus rebukes Peter for the nature and form of his rebuke to Jesus, he is making a statement of fact, not moral judgement: Peter is still seeing through a 'messianic' lens that is causing many people to miss the fact that God's presence is actually among them … and they are completely missing the point. Peter needs to have his mindset reshaped in order to understand 'messiah' as God sees it and, therefore, to be able to comprehend the true identity and mission of Jesus himself.

Most of us reading this exchange between Jesus and Peter are probably glad we are not Peter. But we know something of how the story develops, and we benefit from a sort of theological hindsight. Yet this is strangely encouraging, too. Along with the other disciples, Peter has developed a talent for getting the wrong end of the stick when it comes to understanding Jesus and his mission. He is impetuous and sometimes fickle. But Jesus clearly takes a long-term view of him and his repentance. Jesus knows there is more to come and that Peter's world-view will take more time to begin to be reshaped. And Jesus does not discard Peter for being theologically naïve, backward or stupid.

The reshaping of a world-view or a mindset – especially a rigid religious mindset – does not usually happen instantly. Even Paul's famous encounter with the risen Christ on the road to Damascus was only the beginning of a process of conversion: he then spent three years trying to work out what the truth about the Jesus phenomenon really meant for his world-view, ethics, theology and personal future. Conversion is rarely instantaneous, but always involves a process of constant reshaping. Unfortunately, it is often those of the clearest religious conviction who seem quickest to call others to 'repentance' but slowest to allow themselves to be reshaped.

But Jesus doesn't leave it there. He takes the opportunity to tell his friends and the wider crowds that following him will lead them to the same fate as his. Never one for seducing people into following him, Jesus expects his followers to choose to go with him, fully conscious of the implications. This, of course, would give any PR professional today apoplexy: how could you possibly expect anyone to be attracted to your cause if you tell him or her that it will lead to their death? In a culture that idolises self-fulfilment (browse through the front covers of any magazine shelf in any newsagent), being told to deny your 'self', forgo your rights, openly court your mortality and go on an obscure journey to an end of which you remain ignorant is not exactly sexy. The only people who ever carried their cross were those who were soon to be nailed to it. So, followers of Jesus have to drop their rights to self-fulfilment, lose their romanticism about Christian discipleship and reject any consumer-shaped notion of commitment. Anything else is mere fantasy.

Not everyone faces the sort of dilemmas faced by one writer on the subject of discipleship, but his experience and teaching remain shockingly instructive for all Christians. Dietrich Bonhoeffer was imprisoned by Hitler and finally hanged in Flossenburg nine days before the end of the Second World War. Bonhoeffer could not compartmentalise his faith and let it be conformed to the prevailing (and dehumanising) culture of Nazism. When he wrote his powerful and moving book *The Cost of Discipleship*, he recognised that true discipleship could never be notional and that ethical crises could not simply be contemplated in a library. It was his involvement in the plot to kill Hitler that ultimately sealed his fate, but his opposition to Hitler was fuelled by his powerful conviction that to be a follower of Jesus meant publicly opposing the rule of the Nazis. Faith, politics, economics and ethics were bound together in a theological bundle, inextricably intertwined.

Those who follow Jesus must do so knowingly. They must take responsibility for their choice and their commitment. They must never reserve the right to say that they had been duped into it. And they must realise that such discipleship will always be costly. Jesus gave his friends the time and space to have their understanding of discipleship changed and their perception of his messianic identity reshaped. And that, ultimately, makes the whole business of following Jesus possible: it is a process of conversion to which Jesus calls us, and he does not throw us out of his company when we are slow to grasp it all.

Lord God, give us the grace to see afresh the nature and calling of Jesus, to rediscover in the Scriptures the essential identity of the messiah. As we commit ourselves to follow him, help us to be courageous in intent and patient in expectation … of ourselves and of those who travel with us in his company. Amen.

FRIDAY (LENT 4)

MARK 9:2–13   TRANSFIGURATION

IT is appropriate at this point to remember that the focus of Mark's gospel is twofold: firstly on the identity of Jesus and secondly on the gradual process of recognition by his friends. The first question the reader is meant to ask throughout is: who is this man? The people have been waiting for the return of God's presence to the Temple and have an expectation of what this might look like. God's messiah will be the agent of deliverance, and the people will know that God has come among them when the Romans are kicked out. But is Jesus the one? Or should the people look elsewhere? If Jesus is the messiah, how will the people know? And if he is, then shouldn't he look like the messiah they were expecting?

The second question the reader is meant to ask relates to the friends of Jesus and their gradual (and painful) repentance (change of mindset) during their journey with Jesus from Galilee to Jerusalem, through crucifixion to resurrection and beyond. The agonised process by which they came to understand the identity of Jesus is depicted in the gospel in detail. As we have already observed many times, the disciples misunderstand Jesus, misrepresent him and are slow to work out that it is their concept of 'messiah' that needs to be transformed. They get the wrong end of every stick and give all Christians enormous encouragement by being as fickle and slow as most of us are. Jesus does not discard them, but gives them the time and space to find their way through the disturbing challenges to their prejudices that they face continually.

Following Peter's confession that Jesus is indeed the messiah (but his understanding of what that means is still questionable) and the difficult conversation about the cost of following Jesus, they now go with their leader up a high mountain. While there, they experience something that works at both a real and a metaphorical level for the readers of the text.

The disciples are puzzled and puzzling about who Jesus is, when he is transfigured before their very eyes. He appears to be accompanied by Moses and Elijah, the great prophets and leaders of God's people. But they are seen talking with Jesus, who is then affirmed by the voice of God. It is as if God is trying another way to enlighten their minds, this time by placing Jesus in elevated company and indicating that Jesus completes what Moses and Elijah both prefigured. For example, as Moses led the people of Israel out of captivity in Egypt to freedom in the Promised Land (via a desert), so Jesus will ultimately lead his people (the restored Israel) to their true freedom from captivity to the world and its ways. And if the disciples haven't got the point by now, surely this experience will make the point clear.

The metaphorical element is simply that, as they see the truth about the messianic identity of Jesus, the eyes of their hearts are also opened and enlightened. They see behind the thin curtain that hides the full multi-dimensional reality of God's creation from mortal eyes. But this still doesn't mean they get the point. Mark is keeping us hanging on, waiting for the theological penny to drop in the minds of these disciples. Yet even an encounter with the transfigured Jesus, Moses and Elijah doesn't quite do the trick. It is surely significant of God's infinite patience that he not only identifies Jesus but also urges Peter and his friends to listen to Jesus. Perhaps this was necessary, as Peter has just responded to the vision by offering to build shrines to his religious experience, possibly thus turning it into something fixed and entire of itself.

It is interesting that the journey down the mountain sees Jesus instructing them to keep this experience to themselves until after the resurrection, and the disciples asking questions of him. When we read the gospel narratives straight through (not in little bits), we find that the friends of Jesus are constantly asking him questions. This curiosity seems to characterise discipleship itself. The disciples know no pride in their questioning, but this interrogation seems key to their 'repentance' and understanding. They are doing their theology by questions, not reinforcing their theology by enshrining answers. They find themselves open to new possibilities, but possibly are surprised to find themselves thus.

Jesus might be accused here of confusing Peter and the others unnecessarily. Not only do they have to cope with Moses, Elijah and Jesus' place in the pantheon, but they also have their concept of 'resurrection' queried. They would have assumed that all the righteous would be raised from the dead on the last day; but here Jesus suggests that he will be raised before then and while they are still alive on planet Earth. The concept of messiah is under review for the disciples, and now the received idea of resurrection is being questioned. But, again, Jesus knows that this will only make sense much later when the resurrection has been experienced.

SATURDAY (LENT 4)

MARK 12:35–44   A WIDOW'S MITE

THINGS are not always what they appear to be. And some things in this world are hard to understand without crucial bits of information to which we do not have access at this particular point in time. When we read a gospel such as Mark's, we need to do so as if we didn't know the end of the story. Crucifixion should come as a terrible shock because, according to the received script, the messiah is not supposed to die. Then, out of the devastation comes resurrection, and the friends of Jesus are left to put back together the pieces of their shattered story in a completely new way – one that points to a new reality, a new way of understanding God, the world and people. But we should read the gospel as if we don't know what is coming.

Today we find Jesus teaching in the Temple, and once again he faces us with contrasts. The religious teachers are preoccupied with questions of theology, wondering how the messiah can both be a 'son' and 'Lord'. But Jesus articulates their question without answering it; he simply leaves it hanging in the air. And yet the ordinary people listened to him 'with delight'. Why? Did they enjoy being confused by difficult theological riddles? Or were they just pleased to see the clever religious teachers finding themselves embarrassed by this itinerant upstart from the north country? Well, maybe the clue lies in what follows immediately in Mark's account.

If Jesus wanted to make friends and win influence, he went about it the wrong way. Instead of maintaining a respectful silence in respect of the behavioural contradictions of the powerful people, he publicly holds them up to embarrassing scrutiny. He exposes their hypocrisy and draws attention to their weaknesses. Whereas true religious devotion is to be found in humble and discreet service and sacrifice, these powerful teachers parade their religiosity in the public arena. They want people to see just how pious they are and to evoke admiration for and envy of their spiritual practices. Their business is exercised in demonstrating their popularity in the market place and acquiring the symbols of public status and religious honour. Yet, in doing all this, they are only paying lip service to the God whom they purport to serve and worship. And they obviously haven't read the Old Testament prophets.

Amos is a good prophet to turn to when faced with ostentatious piety. Amos came from Tekoa at a time of religious revival and boldly declared that God hated the worship songs and culture of the people. Why? Because they sang their songs to God while ignoring his nature and priorities. How, Amos asks, can God's people, who bear his name and therefore should reflect his character, possibly praise God in church and at the same time abuse God by 'trampling on the heads of the poor'? How can God's people expect to get away with taking God and his favour for granted while institutionalising injustice in their society and denying the character of God in their public and private life? Amos does not pull his punches in demonstrating that God has some harsh justice to mete out to those who think he is impressed with a show of religious fervour or commitment that is divorced from a true representation of what God is like (merciful) and who God is for (the poor and humble).

There is something of this in Jesus' harsh words directed (to the delight of the crowds) towards those religious leaders who still have not heard or understood the stark challenge of Amos' words. Jesus is clear that only justice and punishment await those who make a show of their spiritual gifts (long, articulate and theologically accurate prayers) while destroying the lives of poor people such as widows and vulnerable people who do not have fancy robes to float around in.

Unless the life we lead reflects the prayers we say, then we are kidding ourselves. The truth of our lives (as James makes clear in his letter) will be seen not in what we choose to demonstrate to our credit, but rather in the way we give priority to caring for the vulnerable and weak of this world – thus fulfilling the call and priorities of God himself as seen in Jesus of Nazareth.

Jesus goes on to push the point home when a widow is seen giving generously of her little while the rich give grandly of their plenty. The implication of the text is that the rich throw in their large amounts so they can be seen while the poor widow simply and discreetly places her little amount into the box. Jesus is clear that the amount is immaterial; the spirit and the cost speak volumes about true love of and devotion to God.

What seems crucial to this episode is the fact that this poor woman, who has no means of support and is of little value in the eyes of society, also has no idea of her value in God's eyes. Unlike those whose giving is characterised by calculation and pride, she has no idea before, during or after her donation that she has done something beautiful for God. She gives out of a generosity of spirit, perhaps even out of thankfulness to God; the rich give a little of their plenty and hope that people will be impressed. Perhaps they think that even God will be impressed. But God, as they would realise if they read prophets such as Amos with any degree of comprehension, cannot be taken for granted; he is not easily impressed with hypocrisy or show.

But it is clear that the truth of who we are and how much we love God is seen not in the amount we give but in the spirit in which we give of our money and our selves. The truth of our values will be seen not in what we sing in church but in the values that shape our behaviour and priorities. If these do not reflect those of God, then we have some changing to do.

Lord God, open our eyes to see the world and its people as you see them. Give us the grace to see and live and give graciously, reflecting the generosity of Jesus towards those who do not know their worth. Amen.

PERSONAL REFLECTION

How can I know that God is both present and sovereign when my life and the lives of those around me are turbulent?

Am I being converted? How do I know?

GROUP DISCUSSION

1. To what extent are our prayers an abdication of responsibility for doing ourselves what we ask God to do for us? Do our prayers and worship songs make God smile or frown (given the warnings of Amos and Jesus)?

2. In what ways can we say that the presence of Jesus diminishes our fear and builds our faith in times of turbulence or threat?

3. How might we describe Jesus and his mission – without using jargon such as 'messiah' – to someone who has never heard of him?

4. In a world dominated by the assumed 'right' to self-fulfilment, why should anyone be expected to deny her- or himself, carry a cross and lose his or her life? Is such a call credible today?

5. How many of our 'mountain-top experiences' lead us to ask questions of God (rather than to enshrine the experience)?

FRIENDS AND ENEMIES

SUNDAY (LENT 5 – PASSIONTIDE)

MARK 6:14–29   HEROD

THERE are Christians today who believe that, if they are faithful to God, all shall (or ought to) go well for them in life. There are even those who peddle a 'gospel' that claims health, wealth and prosperity for those who get the formula right in relation to God and the Church. It is little wonder, then, that such people find themselves facing a crisis of faith when illness or tragedy tears their family apart or unemployment blights their ambitions and self-esteem. Real-life experience has a nasty habit of contradicting stupid and cruel theologies such as those described above.

How anyone can read the Bible and still believe such nonsense is a mystery. Moses the murderer is faithful to God's call to lead the people out of slavery in Egypt to freedom in the Promised Land via forty years wandering in a desert. Yet he dies before getting into the new land, having only glimpsed it. Jeremiah, despite his constantly wishing he hadn't been born and begging God to use someone else as his prophet, is faithful to God in obediently telling the truth to the people. Yet his reward is to go into exile with his people – no special exemption for him. And Jesus promised his friends that if they decided to follow him they would end up carrying a cross – and probably getting nailed to it.

John the Baptiser also found that his faithfulness to God's call and God's word led him not to some sort of consumer paradise but to a prison cell and a brutal execution to satisfy a girl's demand. The real cruelty of John's demise lies in the fact that his death was neither heroic nor dramatic; rather, unaware of what was going on in the party upstairs, he simply heard footsteps coming to his cell before being attacked and beheaded. No final words, no great gestures, no rolls of thunder accompanying his execution: just pain and blood and ignominy. Thus died the faithful prophet who paved the way for the messiah to come.

Reading this story cannot but fill the reader with sadness at the sheer tragedy of the unfolding drama. Herod is a man who is concerned to be seen as the true king of the Jews. Like his father before him, he is concerned about power, status and his place in history. He longs for the popular acclaim that will ensure his place in posterity and guarantee him a safe reign. So the reputation of the wandering prophet from Nazareth inevitably causes him considerable concern. But, rather than going out to kill Jesus and his forerunner, John the Baptiser, Herod finds himself torn between a fascination with the content of John's preaching and his irritation with John's persistence. John has opposed Herod's manipulative marriage to his brother's former wife, Herodias. How can the true king of the Jews behave like this, in a way that makes a mockery of God and his call? But Herod is caught between (1) a recognition that John's message about God and his ways bears the marks of truth and (2) embarrassment about the apparent contradiction between that truth and what was otherwise both personally and politically expedient.

We read that Herod knew John to be a righteous and holy man. But he allows himself to be manipulated by Herodias and her daughter into ordering the execution of this man to satisfy his wife's grudge. And this forms the backdrop to Herod's anxiety about the identity of Jesus. If Jesus is doing extraordinary things and thus being proclaimed a miracle-worker, then Herod has a problem – or, rather, a number of problems. Again Mark is demonstrating that no-one was exempt from facing the question about the identity of Jesus – not even the king. But the problem of identification for Herod is more than a mere curiosity; if Jesus turns out to be John the Baptiser resurrected, then what will that mean for Herod? How will his guilt at the agreement to have John killed be assuaged now that God appears to have vindicated John by bringing him back to life with enhanced powers? What if this Jesus is deemed by the people to be the true king of the Jews? Herod finds himself between a rock and a very hard place. No wonder he is a worried man.

It is easy to be hard on Herod. Political leaders are an easy target for the rest of us, even when our cynicism and accusations are unjust. But there is something authentic about the humanity of Herod here that gives the sensitive reader pause for reflection and self-examination. Herod is caught between the position in which he has found himself in life ... and the desire to have things work out right for him and his people. He knows what is morally right, but walks down a path (in procuring Herodias for his wife) that is destructive of dignity, self-respect and relationships as well as of reputation. He is compelled to listen to the teaching of John the Baptiser and appears to be attracted by what he hears ... but he cannot let go of his securities and fears. A man of power and apparent strength, he is shown to be weak, vacillating between what is right and what is expedient.

No reader should be critical of Herod before recognising that many people face the same dilemmas. Even the Apostle Paul describes a similar destructive bias in Romans 7. It is too easy to point the finger at Herod and people like him, thereby distancing him from the sort of person I might be. But the key to understanding the gospel is the willingness to see in ourselves first the same propensity as that which drove Herod to his own tragedy. He was faced with choices that were too hard to make. He couldn't satisfy everybody and couldn't have everything he wanted. In the end, rather than make a choice, he found himself cornered by competing obligations and found that the decision had been made for him.

By all accounts, Herod was not the sort of man you would want your daughter to marry. But he was a man. And we can recognise in him the sorts of dilemmas and choices we face: between right and wrong, between generosity and fear, between the freedom of a clear conscience and the imprisonment of tortured guilt. Before damning Herod, we must hold him up as a mirror to ourselves.

Lord God, grant us the courage to choose what is right in your eyes and to do what is right in your sight. Save us from the tragedy of indecision and the agony of feeling trapped into making wrong choices. And let us learn from Herod what it is to suffer the consequences of human weakness and failure – help us to embrace the Jesus Herod feared. Amen.

MONDAY (LENT 5 – PASSIONTIDE)

MARK 7:14–30   A SYROPHOENICIAN WOMAN

HUMAN beings have an uncanny knack of missing the point. And Christians are no exception. There are those who become so preoccupied with the Church and how it ought to be that they lose sight of the kingdom of God ... to which the Church is called to point. There are those who become so pedantic about who is 'in' and who is 'out' of the Church that they become blind to the generosity of Jesus as seen in the gospels.

But this is a human problem and not one that is restricted to any single group of people, religious or otherwise. The people of Jesus' time had found themselves down their own blind alley of rules and regulations and appeared to have substituted legal observance for the reality to which that observance had been intended to point. In other words, the means to a greater sense of humanity under God had been confused with the ends; the means had become the end, and the purpose had been lost. Rules that had been shaped to enhance the lives of people in a community had become a prison within which some people lost sight of their true value in God's eyes; the *form* stood in the way of the *content.*

Jesus was doing something extremely challenging when he offered a reinterpretation of the rules regarding the consumption of clean or unclean substances. Religious people religiously kept the rules about what could or could not be touched or consumed. To eat the wrong things would have a spiritual as well as a social consequence, and God could only be pleased by strict adherence to the rules he had given. Jesus, however, says that the rules about cleanliness and purity were designed not as an end in themselves – providing a code by which people could be identified as either 'in' or 'out' – but rather as a pointer to the deeper reality of human motivation and the behaviour that flowed from it. It is not, says Jesus, the food that goes into you that makes you unclean, but the attitudes and actions that come out of you. Eating pork is not the issue; living a life characterised by wickedness, envy and pride *is* the issue.

It is in this context that Jesus encounters a foreign woman on her own territory and finds himself in an interesting situation. He has been saying some controversial things, and the religious authorities are not happy. His reappraisal of the Jewish laws is threatening not only to the received orthodoxy about how life should be lived and society organised, but it also deeply threatens the religious and political status quo. After all, where will it all end if people just stop doing what they are told and we lose the symbols of social cohesion as codified by the hierarchy? So, Jesus leaves his own territory and slips over the border into a Gentile town where he can withdraw from the fray for a while. It might just give the authorities the space and time to cool down a little.

Mark's readers have to remember that Jesus perceives his ministry in terms of calling Jews back to their original vocation: to be the people of God for the sake of the world. This is a ministry to Jews, for these are the people who have the stories and the vocabulary and need to rediscover their roots and the character of their God. They are the ones who need to hear that their long-awaited moment of deliverance is now upon them, that the presence of God has returned and that their exile has now passed. There is an urgency about the Jews hearing and receiving this good news, and Jesus is unwilling to be distracted from this clear priority. The Gentiles will hear and respond to the good news of God in Christ once the Jewish mission has been fulfilled; but that time is not yet here.

So, Jesus attempts to hide away for a while, but finds himself exposed again very quickly. His reputation preceding him, a Gentile woman finds out where he is and presents him with a challenge. Her daughter is unwell, possessed by a spiritual malaise, and she wants Jesus to deliver her. Instead of responding in a kind way (or so it seems), Jesus distinguishes between the 'children' (the Jews) and the 'dogs' (the Gentiles). The woman sharply takes his distinction and turns it on him in a way that impresses Jesus and causes him to recognise the woman's integrity of faith. She leaves to find her daughter at home healed and well.

This encounter is significant for Mark because it places Jesus and the expansion of his mission to all people at the heart of the narrative. Towards the end of the gospel, it is a centurion – another Gentile – who recognises the identity of Jesus as he dies on the cross at Golgotha. The statement is clear: what the Jews are failing to grasp is being grasped by those who are not Jews. Or, to go back to the language of purity, the 'unclean' grasp what the 'clean' don't see. Or, to put it more bluntly, the ethnic or religious origin doesn't matter; it is the grasping of the truth about God and his grace that transforms a person and fulfils their longing for God and his healing.

This might not seem to be a very hard thing to grasp for contemporary Christians. But it is easy for us to underestimate the change of mindset (repentance) that would be required by good Jews of Jesus' time on hearing his message. One way to think about it might be for a Christian to consider how he or she would respond to being told by the preacher that the cross is no longer necessary and that the resurrection is simply a metaphor for a new beginning. Many Christians get very angry when things they hold to be intrinsic to the gospel appear to be questioned. Yet, what Jesus was asking the Jews to do was to undergo a revolution in the way they saw God, the world and people – and this revolution would turn their lives upside down. The consequences would be unimaginable and uncontrollable. And – what was most scary – if wrong, God would never forgive them for their wilful sinfulness. The cost of heeding Jesus' message was potentially very high.

Christians need always to be open to respecting the cost of 'repentance'. Indeed, if Christians appear to be unwilling themselves to be open to having their theological world-view questioned and reshaped, how dare they expect it of anybody else? Surely a Christian should be someone who has experienced the fearful danger of repentance and understands with great sensitivity what it might cost for others to begin such a precarious process. Repentance is not cheap and it is not easy; on the contrary, it is radical (literally, goes to the very roots of who and how we are) and costly. It should not be commended lightly, and it should always be illustrated openly in those who claim to follow the Jesus who went to the heart of the human condition, exposing its contradictions and inviting a courageous response.

Lord God, before I judge the unwillingness of others to 'change their mind', help me to have the humility and grace to discern if mine needs to be changed first. Help me to be like Jesus in perceiving the importance of the reality over the symbolic, the content over the form. Amen.

TUESDAY (LENT 5 – PASSIONTIDE)

MARK 8:11–21   PHARISEES

IF 'missing the point' was the starting point for yesterday's reflection, then it is also pertinent to today's. In one sense, Mark's gospel is an illustration – over several years and in a range of different contexts with diverse groups of people – of just how easy it is to miss the point of who Jesus is and what he is about, especially (and ironically) for those who are closest to him.

Remember that this is a people who have been longing and praying and looking for the coming of the messiah, the one whose activity and proclamation would signify the end of Israel's exile and the vindication of their identity and story. They would know that God was among them again and the Roman occupation would be over. But Jesus has come proclaiming that the kingdom is in fact already here among them ... in him. From the very beginning of his public ministry, he calls on his people to repent (change their way of seeing) and believe the good news (commit themselves to the implications and consequences of what they now see through their new eyes). As we have seen, though, the rest of the gospel is a sort of illustration or explication of what it looks like for the kingdom to have come, for God to be present among his people in his messiah: there is healing, reconciliation, proclamation in word and deed of good news for people who have got used to seeing and hearing very bad news. And we have seen that two questions then dominate the text: (1) who is this Jesus, and is he really the messiah? And (2) who 'sees' and who doesn't?

It is possible to read the gospel as a joke with a punchline that comes at the beginning followed by a long attempt to explain or illustrate it to people who 'just don't get it'. Of course, whereas a joke dies once the teller tries to explain it, the gospel comes alive as the journey progresses and all the wrong people get the point ... in contrast to those who should have got it right at the outset.

Consider the context. Jesus has engaged in a dispute with the Pharisees about the purity laws and what should constitute 'clean' and 'unclean'. Unlike the Pharisees, Jesus sees through and beyond the rules to the human response that the rules are meant to point towards; he sees the rules as the servant, not the master of the kingdom. Having had this encounter with the Pharisees and said some radical and disturbingly seditious things, Jesus tries to disappear and lie low for a while in a Gentile town. But there he is sought out by a non-Jewish woman who engages with him on the matter of where Gentiles fit into Jesus' vision. Her daughter is healed, demonstrating conclusively that Jesus' messiahship is not the sole property of the Jews themselves – that God is coming to rescue all people of whatever ethnic and religious origin. Jesus then returns to his own territory and heals a deaf and mute man – effectively enabling one who has thus far been unable to hear good news and tell it to become an evangelist to his own people. The kingdom is here – see for yourselves the evidence of its presence! Jesus then feeds 4,000 people – giving bread to the hungry and symbolising that he is feeding the sheep in a way that those whose job and calling it is to be 'good shepherds' have failed to do.

There is here both an implicit and an explicit contrast between Jesus and those who should be leading the people to and with God. But the charge is unavoidable: the teachers of the people have themselves consistently missed the point of their calling, their faith and their religious observance, thus mistaking the means for the end and confusing a concern for God with pedantry for rules. The tragedy is as poignant as any other character whose seemingly inevitable demise unfolds before us on a stage – Macbeth, for instance. We watch, longing to make the connection for the 'blind' tragic character; but we cannot do it for him.

All of this underlies the encounters Jesus has with the Pharisees. Nowhere does he condemn them for being Pharisees – indeed, it is possible that Jesus was himself a Pharisee. But the tragedy that repeats itself and eventually builds to a brutal climax lies in the fact that it is the very people who should 'see' and help others to 'see' who appear to be blind and either unwilling or unable to open themselves to a change in the way they see God, the world and themselves (repentance).

The Pharisees are intrigued by Jesus and clearly have an interest in following him around. They are persistent in trying to engage him in theological argument, trying, it seems, to trip him up or find his theological Achilles heel. Jesus is wary of the game they are playing, but does not hide his explicit views about them from them. He is forthright in his critique of their failure to fulfil their vocation and their unwillingness to recognise that for which they have longed and prayed for so many generations. It is a bit like the story told to me by a rabbi friend: at the end of the Passover celebration in the synagogue, he went to throw open the doors to see if the messiah had come and found a drunk tramp urinating on the steps. He immediately slammed the doors shut ... before being haunted by the fear that, if this had actually been the messiah, he had just shut him out. How, he said, would I recognise the messiah anyway? And does he have to fit my prejudiced expectation?

The Pharisees get a hard time in the gospels, and we can understand why. Jesus doesn't play subtle word games with them; rather, he blasts them with unequivocal criticism – probably because he knows that time is short and no other form of communication is likely to get through their blind prejudices. But the Pharisees are not the only people to find it hard to get the point about Jesus. We Christians of the twenty-first century have equal difficulty in being consistent and demonstrate an equal talent for missing the point. Jesus demonstrates mercy and grace where we want to know who is 'in' and who is 'out' of the Church. Jesus collects a ragbag of followers and compels them to walk with him *and each other* ... whereas we want to exclude those who differ from us in the slightest nuances of doctrine or practice. We ask God for a sign of his presence and favour ... and ignore the message of the gospels that screams out from the text: what further signs do you need than what you see here in Jesus? The kingdom is come, and the evidence is public.

Lord God, open our eyes to see in Jesus the face of God, in the hands of Jesus the touch of God, in the voice of Jesus the word of God and in the heart of Jesus the priorities of God for the world. Amen.

WEDNESDAY (LENT 5 – PASSIONTIDE)

MARK 8:22–30   PETER

FOR people who are only too aware of their potential for failure and their talent for missing the point, Peter is a great hero. Peter's name means 'rock', and most people's assumption (based on Matthew's account) is that the rock is some sort of granite. But reading the gospel accounts of Peter leads us to imagine a different sort of substance – sandstone, for example. Peter is constantly being shaped, reshaped, hurt, bewildered, enthused and challenged. And this doesn't stop after the crucifixion or resurrection … or even after Pentecost. Peter is supremely human and illustrates well what it means to walk with Jesus into the unknown future, trusting only that there is always more to learn and discover.

Peter is also being contrasted by Mark with the Pharisees. They are stubbornly unable or unwilling to 'see' who Jesus is and what he is about; Peter, on the other hand, does 'see', but only partially understands what he sees.

Jesus takes his friends on a long journey to the slopes of a northern mountain. They have just witnessed what they too are going to experience in a different sort of way: a blind man has his sight restored, at first seeing unclearly, but later seeing clearly. Peter and his friends see something of who Jesus is and what he is about, but they haven't yet faced the clear implications of this identification. They have been with him and seen the signs of God's kingdom among them in healing and proclamation of good news. But they have only slowly been fitting this into a reshaped mindset or world-view. Now Jesus brings them to a place where they must answer for themselves who they think he is. Remember, thus far in the narrative they have witnessed Jesus 'proclaiming' the kingdom of God; now they are going to have to face the notion that Jesus thinks of himself as the king, the true King of the Jews. This is perhaps a more radical step-change than we might think today.

This conversation is the crucial point both in the journey of these disciples with Jesus and in Mark's narrative. We have listened to Jesus, seen his healings and heard his teachings. Furthermore, we have witnessed the growing conflict between Jesus and the religious authorities in the land. We get the clear impression that this journey is not to be open-ended but heading towards a climax when the forces of opposition will come head to head with Jesus and his friends. But even Jesus knows he cannot run before the disciples can walk.

It must have been tempting for Jesus to blurt the whole story out right at the beginning and challenge the people to either accept or reject him. But he doesn't. Instead, he allows his friends the time and space to see and think and talk and explore. He doesn't rush them, for he knows that they have to work all this stuff out for themselves. It is vital that each disciple takes responsibility for his own discipleship, making and owning his own judgements about the identity and mission of Jesus. As we saw earlier in this book, 'repentance' is a process that takes time and will not be rushed.

So, Jesus finally faces them with the hard question: who do people say that I am? What judgement are other people making about my identity? In this sense, it is easy for the disciples to respond; they are simply reporting what they have heard. But then Jesus denies them a hiding place behind the judgements of other people and invites them to own their own decision: 'Who do you say I am?' And now the friends of Jesus, who have watched and listened and shared in this remarkable journey, still ignorant of what lies ahead, voice at last their conclusion: Peter, on their behalf, says: 'You are the messiah'.

What is interesting here, however, is that Peter's understanding of what 'messiah' means is still shaped by his traditional Jewish perception. He is concluding that Jesus is 'messiah', but does not go on to explain what he thinks this means. In other words, he makes his judgement, still not fully grasping the import of what he is saying … and Jesus takes it for what it is. Peter and the others have now concluded that Jesus is the long-awaited messiah, but they still have some way to go in reshaping what that means. At this point, it almost certainly does not include being executed on a Roman gallows.

Peter's story will continue, and it doesn't get any more glorious as time goes by. He will go on to misunderstand Jesus' prediction of death, will fail to grasp the agony of Jesus in Gethsemane, will disown Jesus when the heat is on and will abandon him to his lonely fate. The last we will hear of Peter is when the three women are told by the empty tomb to go and tell the disciples and Peter (specifically by name) that Jesus has been raised and will meet them again in Galilee.

It is not surprising that many Christians find new hope in Peter's story. He is happy to make great protestations of faith while demonstrating more enthusiasm than understanding. He does not understand himself and his own limitations, but he presses on regardless. He is weak at the very point where he thinks he is strongest, and has to face the truth about himself in the most painful way. Peter is the sort of 'rock' that is shaped by the elements and not inured to them; he is more sandstone than granite.

The remarkable thing here, though, is that Jesus never despises Peter for his weakness or inconsistency, for his ignorance or partial grasp of the truth. Indeed, Jesus makes space for him and gives him the time to learn for himself and make his own mind up about who Jesus is and what he is about. In that sense, Peter is the archetypical disciple: one who journeys with Jesus and others (whom Jesus and not he has chosen), making mistakes, not grasping the whole truth, failing both himself and Jesus ... but still being embraced by Jesus and not excluded.

If the Church is truly the Body of this Christ, surely it should reflect this generosity.

Lord God, thank you for Peter and the encouragement that he brings to us as ordinary disciples of Jesus. Help us to see, to learn, to journey together, growing in faith and understanding as we go. Amen.

THURSDAY (LENT 5 – PASSIONTIDE)

MARK 10:17–31   A RICH YOUNG MAN

JESUS has been teaching that there are some surprising differences between people's perceptions of what God's kingdom and God's messiah will look like and the reality. Contrary to the notion that those who obey every jot and tittle of the Law will be assured God's special favour, Jesus takes a child and tells the crowds that being like a child is the only way to enter God's kingdom. But what is a child? Certainly, a young child is not usually overly concerned with religious pedantry or the accumulation of wealth. But a child surely is unencumbered by the complicating consumerism of adulthood according to which the value of a person can consciously or unconsciously be reckoned by his or her wealth. Indeed, for the people of Jesus' time, accumulated wealth was regarded as evidence of God's blessing. Once again, Jesus invites people to see differently.

The young child who exemplifies the characteristics necessary for admission to the kingdom (curiosity, playful lack of inhibition, taking people as they are and so on) is then contrasted with a young man who approaches Jesus in all seriousness. Clearly there is a buzz going around about Jesus, and many of the bright young people of his day wanted to meet him and question him. Unlike the Pharisees and other religious leaders, this young man is not trying to trip Jesus up or lure him into saying something he might regret. This young man is serious about his faith, his theological commitment and his ethics, and approaches Jesus with honour and respect. So, he kneels at Jesus' feet and asks him the million-dollar question.

'Eternal life' speaks not of quantity of years, but of quality of existence. The big question for Jews had less to do with definition than access: how do I become certain that eternal life will be mine? Now, it is probable that the young man expected to be given some variation on a well-worn theme: fulfil the rules and regulations as laid down by a particular group (Pharisees, Sadducees or Essenes, for example), and you will be assured of your ultimate vindication before and by God. But Jesus doesn't do this. Instead, he cites a number of the Commandments and then sums them all up by enjoining the young man to let nothing come between him and God's call. But what is interesting is how Jesus responds to the man's initial protestation that he has kept all the laws since childhood. Whereas you and I might think he was a self-righteous creep, Jesus looks hard at him and 'loves him'. In other words, Jesus respects the seriousness of the man's devotion and commitment and does not despise or question it. He takes the man as he is.

However, Jesus then turns the screw. Obeying the ethical commandments (regarding theft, fraud, murder and so on) is manageable; but, when it comes to removing idols and freeing ourselves from those things that shield the heart from God, then the matter becomes more difficult. This is a man who has not known what it is to be vulnerable or dependent on other people. His life is as cushioned as it can be, and to ask him voluntarily to surrender his wealth is to ask a great deal. But this is where the rubber hits the road for this particular man. Is he able and willing to leave behind those things that will militate against him being able to stay the course of discipleship? Jesus is going to a cross, and the heat is going to be on his friends at a time of great pressure and distress. During this time, it is essential that the disciples depend on each other, unafraid of their vulnerability and interdependence. Someone who wants to protect his independence will not be able to cope with this.

We must note, however, that Jesus is not being unnecessarily harsh or judgemental towards the young man; he is simply being realistic and refusing to allow the young man to live with illusions. As we noted earlier, Jesus never seduced anyone into following him and always made his disciples own their own discipleship. If they decided to follow Jesus, they did so of their own choosing, and they would bear their own clear responsibility for the choices they had made. This was going to prove vitally important when the brutal pressure was on them and they could not simply blame Jesus for misleading them with fake promises.

The young man goes away a sad man. I wonder if he ever came back again? We don't know the end of this particular story; we just get this snapshot of his encounter with Jesus. But it is worth noting also that Jesus does not run after him, inviting him to pay by instalments or give more money to the Church. This whole business is not about amounts of cash or quantities of stuff. Rather, it is primarily about being honest about those things (they usually are things, but might also be relationships) that inhibit our relationship with God and our openness to live freely in and for the sake of his kingdom in the world.

To paraphrase Frederick Buechner's paraphrase of Jesus: 'It is easier to get a Rolls Royce through a revolving door than for a rich man to enter the kingdom of God'. Wealth and stuff, rather than being a sign of God's blessing, more often prove to be a tempting diversion from dependence on God and his people. Wealth is not intrinsically wrong, but it can do damage to the soul of even the most serious disciple of Jesus.

The disciples have left everything to go on this journey with Jesus, and Jesus introduces to them the revolutionary notion that those who follow him, having left homes, goods, relationships and so on, will find themselves in a new family, with new relationships of mutual sharing and trust. Jesus conspicuously does not promise that all will go well for them – as a sort of reward for special discipleship – and states that they will share all things, including persecution. The road will be rough, and the rewards will not necessarily be experienced in this life; but, even in the midst of all this, they will experience a dimension of shared life and journey that will bring its own reward.

Discipleship has not changed, and Jesus' call has not changed. The only question remains as it did for the rich young man: how serious am I about facing the cost of following Jesus and taking my place in the company of his fellow-travellers?

Lord God, give to your people the grace to put you before all else. Grant us the courage to give ourselves to your people and for your people in order that together we might experience your life in our common life. Amen.

FRIDAY (LENT 5 – PASSIONTIDE)

MARK 10:32–45   JAMES AND JOHN

SOMETIMES we hear Christians romanticising about the early Church and pleading that if only we could get back to the patterns of the New Testament Church everything in the ecclesiastical garden would be lovely. This is the stuff of fantasy. There was no Golden Age of the Church. There has never been a time when the Church or a church hasn't been arguing about something, been dividing over some doctrine or practice or seen particular elements vying for power and influence. So, we would do well to reject romantic fantasy and get on with the job in the real world and real church to which God has, in his reckless grace and wild imaginative love, called us to share.

If the Acts of the Apostles does not convince you of this, and the fact that Paul and his colleagues had to write so many questioning, indignant, sarcastic and corrective letters to various churches doesn't make you think again, then the current passage will surely do the trick.

James and John have been with Jesus from the very beginning of his public ministry. They, along with Peter and the others, have watched and listened and stuck with Jesus and his friends all the way so far. So, we might be forgiven for thinking that they have at least understood *something* of Jesus' new perspective on

God, the world and people. Well, it appears not to be the case. To read on is to discover with some degree of relief that Jesus' friends were as messy as the Church is now and that stubborn ignorance of essential doctrine does not disqualify us from the ranks of the disciples of Jesus.

Jesus asks James and John what it is they want him to do for them. They reply with a bid for glory – the high positions of governance and status when Jesus eventually takes his place as king. Yet they have no idea what they are asking for. They have singularly failed to understand that this is not what the kingdom is about. Indeed, the problem with Israel that has led them into this long exile was precisely the problem behind this question: they took their 'chosenness' as status and privilege instead of responsibility and self-sacrifice for the sake of the world – including the Gentiles.

But Jesus does not despise them for this gross ignorance. He doesn't bewail their stupidity or ram home to them the right answer to his question about them. No, he recognises that people have to come to the realisation of who he is and what he is about in their own time and in their own terms. They have to discover for themselves what the kingdom is all about, not simply be told the right answers by an impatient messiah. So, he gives them a cryptic response in which the brothers expose their ignorance and ambitious bravado again.

Isn't it interesting, though, that the other disciples are not impressed? And isn't this totally true to our own experience of life in the Church? The other disciples get wind of James and John's request (but we are not told how or who told them about it), and they are furious. Why? Is their fury because they almost got trumped by the two brothers and nearly lost out

161

on their own places of status? Or is it because they see more clearly that the disciples belong together and must refrain from selfish ambition within the group? Or is it because they resent one or two of the group playing surreptitious political games behind the backs of their rivals? Well, we cannot be sure.

However, we can be sure that when Jesus has finished with them they are chastened – even if they still don't quite get the point. Jesus hits the issue head on: in the kingdom of God, all are servants, and greatness is to be found in generous self-giving for the sake of others. So, common notions of power, status and 'ownership' of the group (or the Church) have to be consciously and willingly rejected in favour of the harder way of humility.

It is worth remembering here what we noted earlier in this book, that Mark is trying to tell us something powerful about Jesus. James and John are people who have been close to Jesus and should, therefore, see clearly the truth about the kingdom of God and the identity of Jesus. But they are still blind. Yet Jesus goes on from here to ask blind Bartimaeus the same question he asked James and John. Bartimaeus (the sinner) has his sight restored. Mark is telling us that the blind see what the seeing are blind to. The kingdom of God is shocking and subversive of so many of our pet assumptions and our arrogance.

This encounter between Jesus and the two brothers is striking for the reasons mentioned above. But it is also notable for another reason which isn't immediately visible: Jesus is laying down a political gauntlet which will soon be picked up and used to force his torture and execution.

Jesus and his friends are now on their journey towards Jerusalem, where the messianic claims will be tested. Jesus knows what lies ahead for him there, but his friends still can't conceive of the messiah dying without this being a contradiction in terms. The disciples expect to enter Jerusalem in glory, ready to take power and implement the new age of Jesus' reign as king. But Jesus knows that his entry into Jerusalem will cause such political fear on the part of the authorities that his action and presence will be taken as politically provocative. Those who will sit at his right and left hand will not be occupying places of governance and privilege, but will most probably be nailed to a gallows.

Mark does not allow us to escape into private piety when reading his gospel. Jesus' ministry is public, his message subversive, his challenge political and his demise inevitable.

Lord God, open our eyes that we might see as Jesus does the true way of God's kingdom. Preserve us from mistaking worldly notions of power for godly notions of service. Set us free to accompany Jesus into Jerusalem, there confronting the powers of our world with the presence of God's judging love. Amen.

SATURDAY
(LENT 5 – PASSIONTIDE)

MARK 15:1–15   PILATE AND THE ROMANS

IF Herod craved recognition as king of the Jews, Pilate just wanted a quiet life. It was bad enough being consigned to an outpost of the Roman Empire such as this anyway, but the constant uprisings, mini-revolutions and petty intrigues with local leaders made life for Pilate the Procurator fairly uncomfortable. He could be forgiven for just wanting the trouble to go away, for the local people just to accept Roman rule and all the benefits that that would bring. But every day there seemed to be fresh problems to address and new rebels to crucify. All Pilate really seems to have wanted was a quiet life in the colonies before returning in glory to Rome.

Pilate and his armies are used to revolts and would-be messiahs attempting to lead the ultimate uprising against the occupation. Rome's way of dealing with such trouble was simply to crucify the ringleaders and their followers, making an example of them, warning the ordinary populace of what happens to people who challenge the might of the Roman Empire. But Jesus is leading a different sort of revolution. He is a different sort of messiah. And Pilate doesn't really want to be bothered with him. He just wants the latest problem solved with the least amount of hassle.

When Jesus enters Jerusalem and eventually is brought before the Roman court, something very dramatic is happening. Jesus, disowned by his own people's leaders, now finds himself confronting the power of Rome. But Jesus, having accepted Pilate's attribution to him of the title 'King of the Jews', refuses to answer any other charges brought against him. Accusations are made, but his response is to keep silence. After all, Pilate might think that Jesus is on trial here; but Jesus is by his very presence putting the might of Rome on trial instead. It is appropriate to render to Caesar what is Caesar's (12:13–17); but Caesar and his brutal regime now stand in the place of God's judgement. Rome might take away his life and his blood, but Rome cannot displace the presence of God – even here in the most dreadful place of threat, danger and horror.

Pilate wants to maintain the popular peace – and, although he finds no fault in Jesus, he is unwilling to let justice get in the way of expediency. If the people want Jesus' blood, then they shall have it … if, by giving them what they want, it will keep the people calm and controllable. Jesus might pose a theological challenge to the Jewish leaders and teachers, but Pilate is interested only in maintaining the political peace. As soon as Jesus acknowledges that he is content to be called 'King of the Jews', Pilate smells trouble. He does not want a power battle breaking out between Herod and a trumped-up pretender such as Jesus from Nazareth. Just keep things tidy and quiet; give the powermongers what they want; prevent riots and don't let your authority be undermined in any way.

There is, however, a further element to Pilate's encounter with Jesus. The Passover is being celebrated by the Jews, and this always spells trouble for the

Roman overlords. Passover is that festival when the Jews relive the exodus, that deliverance from Egyptian oppression by the initiative of God himself. This is the archetypical story against which Israel measures itself and understands its place in the world. God liberated his people from their slavery once, and he will do it again. At each Passover celebration, the agony of oppression and the joy of liberation are remembered and relived. The people then cannot but help look forward to that day when they will once again be set free from their imprisonment in their own land. And this means that the political and religious temperature in the country rises considerably at the time of this festival. Hopes are stirred and passions aroused. These are the conditions in which hot-headed young men find their idealism stirred and their loins strengthened for the fight.

Pilate is acutely aware of all this. So, it makes sense for him to deal quickly with Jesus and get the immediate problem sorted. He obviously didn't see Jesus as a serious threat in terms of normal messianic pretensions: he didn't round up all Jesus' followers and nail them all to crosses at Golgotha.

In the background of all this ferment, there is another story being told. Pilate thinks the whole business is about political stability and the Pax Romana, but Jesus knows that the Empire of Death is now being confronted by the Prince of Peace. Rome might speak of peace, but it maintained peace by exercising the most brutal forms of execution and torture against anyone who dared to threaten or question the powerful. The Roman world could not but proclaim that Caesar is Lord of the world; Jesus now silently begins a confrontation that will expose Caesar as an impostor who cannot get away with usurping what belongs only to God himself. Even the Roman Empire itself will soon discover in the most surprising way that this messiah refuses to let death have the final word and destruction ultimate power.

It is possible to feel a certain sympathy for Pilate as he is caught between a desire for justice and the demands of political or social expediency. But he is clear where his priorities lie, and justice will simply have to take a back seat for a while. After all, one more crucifixion isn't going to change the world, is it? But one more riot might just change his life by disturbing the social status quo. So, Pilate nonchalantly waves his hand and consigns Jesus to his death, not realising that he is about to be humiliated by the failure of Rome's ultimate weapon – fear and death – to get rid of Jesus once and for all.

Pilate represents an empire that feeds on arrogance and power. Jesus represents a kingdom that will not be bound by the rules of the empire or the threats that the empire can issue. Empires come and go, but the God who is present in this Jesus is not to be displaced by Caesar or Pilate or anybody else ... even by an instrument of torture, fear and death.

Lord God, where expediency threatens to outweigh the call for justice in our own world, may your people have the courage to confront those with power. Help us to get our vision right, our priorities in line with yours, our hearts fired with your love. Amen.

PERSONAL REFLECTION

Reflecting on the story of John the Baptiser, how can I know that God is there when everything appears to be going wrong for me?

What is the likely cost to me of having my mindset reshaped by Jesus and the proclamation of his kingdom?

GROUP DISCUSSION

1. Do we feel any sympathy for Herod or Pilate?

2. What sort of rock is the Church built on – granite or sandstone?

3. How can we be sure we are not 'Pharisees', constantly missing the point about Jesus?

4. If discipleship demands mutual interdependence between all followers of Jesus, how might this be expressed in the life of a church or a group of churches? How might this involve making space for each other to be disciples-under-construction in a messy (rather than tidy) church?

5. What do we think would count as evidence of God's blessing in the life of a Christian, a church or a community?

ENDINGS AND BEGINNINGS

PALM SUNDAY (HOLY WEEK)

MARK 11:1–11 ENTERING JERUSALEM

FOR people who can travel from one part of the globe to another by hopping on an aeroplane, it is hard to imagine what it was like to travel in first-century Palestine. Coming from Jericho, the lowest place on earth, to Jerusalem was hard and dramatic. From the arid depths of the desert, the traveller would have to climb nearly 4,000 feet to reach the holy city. The journey would not be easy and it would not be quick. When Jesus and his friends made that last journey together, they had ample time for thinking, musing, conversing and debating as they went on their way. The physical journey was mirrored by another sort of journey.

Jesus has set his face towards Jerusalem, and they aim to arrive there in time for the Passover. But we can only understand the power of this if we understand the context in which the events of the next few days are to take place. Jerusalem is the heart of the political and religious establishment, the locus of all that Jewish people hope for. The Temple is there – the physical reminder of God's presence and God's promise. It is here that Rome will have to be taken on and defeated at last. It is here, in this city, that the messiah will lead God's people to victory over the oppressor and the ultimate vindication of their history.

So, the journey to the city is long and hard, and yet the reward of being there will be immense. But add into this the atmosphere of Passover – the great celebration of liberation from Egyptian oppression – and we can just begin to comprehend the excitement and fervent emotions that will move the people to imagine a new future. Is this the time God will return to his people and set them free? Is it this year that the messiah will appear and identify himself before the people? Is it this time that the course of history will be irrevocably changed and God's sovereignty over the entire world be finally recognised – even by the pagan Gentiles?

The friends of Jesus are not only caught up in this frenzy of excited aspiration, but they also overlay it with their enthusiastic endorsement of Jesus as that present messiah. They have begun to see and grasp the possibility that Jesus is the true King of the Jews, the one called by God to take control and drive the pagans out of the holy places. However, their comprehension of what this actually means is still very limited, and they find themselves mixed up in a complex of competing ideas and hopes. If Jesus is a king, should he not ride into the city in a blaze of glory?

Certainly, Jesus behaves like a king: he claims the right to appropriate someone else's colt as if it were his natural sovereign place to do so. Then he rides into the city from the Mount of Olives, all the time sensing both the excitement of the journey and the fear of what lies ahead of him there. The people who welcome him do so in terms reserved for kings: laying a carpet of clothing in front of his path and waving branches of acclaim and welcome. This is David's city and the place where David's kingdom will once again be established. But Jesus knows, as the people do not, that he is a different sort of king, coming to establish a different sort of kingdom. He is going to seriously disappoint people whose expectations of him and the nature of 'kingship' will now be subverted by him. They wave their branches and shout their hosannas, but they do not know what they are doing.

Jerusalem, the city on the hills, is welcoming the king ... and missing the point. The same people who now shout his acclaim will shortly shout for his blood, and those who wave their branches in celebration will soon be waving their fists in anger as the Roman torturers get ready for work. There is a deep irony in this scene, and that irony is going to prove ultimately tragic. We can only imagine the agony for Jesus of knowing that two narratives are running concurrently here and that they cannot be held together: the one that suggests that the messiah will assert his power by evicting the Romans, and the one that sees the messiah in terms of the man who will fulfil the fundamental call of Israel from Abraham onwards – to give up his life for the sake of the world. According to the first narrative, the concepts of 'messiah' and 'death' are contradictory; according to the second, 'messiah' will only fulfil his calling and be recognised by 'his death'.

It is a feature of Mark's sense of the dramatic that, just as events seem to be speeding up towards the climax of Jesus' ministry and life, Jesus stops. He has entered the city, but then all he does is go to the Temple, have a look around (which he must have done a hundred times before) ... and leave to stay the night elsewhere. So, what is that all about? Well, the poignancy is acute here. Jesus is about to fulfil what the Temple has failed to do. Yet, here in the Temple he will find his people failing to grasp the heart of God's call – precisely what the Temple was supposed to remind them of – and feel the heat of their frustrated

171

expectations and the pain of their blind rejection. No wonder he goes there quietly, looks around and muses on what it has all come to.

Before condemning those who acclaimed Jesus before changing their tune later, I would want to ask where I would have found myself in this story. Surely, fickle affections and short-lived commitments are not the sole preserve of the people of Jerusalem in AD 33. The terrible truth of this bewildering entry into the city is that ordinary, good, hopeful religious people are easily swayed in their convictions by the loud voices of powerful people, by the power of expediency and short-term gain, by the apparently persuasive reasoning of parties that ally with each other in unholy ways in order to achieve their ignoble ends. Jews and Gentiles will come together to eliminate a potential problem.

I don't know if I would have been any different from those people of Jerusalem. I am not sure I am different.

Lord God, grant us open and honest hearts that we might see the truth about ourselves and our own fragile devotion to you and your kingdom. Teach us the need for genuine humility when considering the failures of others to be consistent in their commitment to you. Amen.

MONDAY (HOLY WEEK)

MARK 11:12–25   CLEANSING THE TEMPLE

IT is a fact of human nature – even Christian human nature – that we shape God in our own image. And, in that respect, we are no different from the people of Jesus' time who thought that he couldn't possibly be the messiah because he neither looked the part nor followed the expected script. It is far easier for us today to get sentimental over the baby in the manger than to cope with the bleeding man on the gallows. It proves more personally satisfying – or, at least, less disturbing – to see Jesus as 'gentle, meek and mild' rather than as angry, violent or 'unnecessarily difficult'.

Once again, we have to read this passage in two ways at the same time, for it is rich in symbolism as well as drama. In the Bible, the fig tree is a symbol of Israel, the people called by God to bear fruit to nurture the world (Abraham's calling was that all peoples of the world should be blessed through him). And Jesus finds a fig tree that is useless because it is fruitless. It has no purpose any longer and might as well not be there – except to remind people of its sad demise. So, he does to it what he will later do in and to the Temple: he condemns it. It might seem an untimely judgement given that it isn't even the season for figs, but time has now run out.

And this is precisely what he thinks of the Temple, the ultimate symbol of Israel's national life. Instead of being the place that would bring the people to a constant recognition of their calling and purpose in the world, it had become all that the prophets had warned against. In Jeremiah 7, the people are condemned for taking God for granted. Jeremiah expresses God's anger and frustration at a people who have reduced their glorious vocation to a miserable mantra of self-satisfied wishful thinking: 'The temple of the Lord, the temple of the Lord, the temple of the Lord'. This place that is supposed to be for the blessing of the world – all the world – has become a token of narrow nationalist pretensions; and what is intended to symbolise the character of a just and merciful God has now become a veneer of religious complacency under which injustice and immorality can flourish.

Jesus knows his Bible and picks up on this damning judgement as he turns his fury towards this abused place. The fact that the Temple precincts were used for commercial activity is not the point here – despite much popular preaching of this text. The point of the quotation is not that the Temple should be a house of prayer (as opposed to a commercial outlet for local businesses), but that it should be a house of prayer 'for all nations'. In other words, it is to be not a place of refuge and defensiveness for the Jews alone but the source of nurture, blessing and service for all people of the world that is God's. The failure of the people to use the Temple appropriately has led to this stark demonstration of condemnation by Jesus.

But it actually goes further than this. Jesus can see the writing on the wall for his people and their Temple. Their unbending fixation on the military expulsion of the Romans from their land has missed the point of their fundamental calling, and their consequent failure to grasp what 'messiah' is all about has blinded them to the likely consequences of their passion for liberation. Jesus is not the sort of king who will rise up against the Roman Empire and lead a violent revolution; that way lies bloodshed, the perpetuation of that dreadful cycle of violence, retribution and vengeance. But, if the people persist in pursuing the nationalist agenda, all the while failing to grasp the nature of God's call to them, the only end will be destruction. And, as in previous centuries when exile followed failure, the concrete symbols of God's presence, promise and favour will be taken from them. Not only will the pagans desecrate the holy Temple, they will destroy it. And, in AD 70, this is exactly what happened.

Jesus can see what lies ahead. Like the prophets of the Old Testament, he sees behind the appearance of solidity and permanence and identifies the seeds of inevitable destruction. God will not be mocked or taken for granted by his own people. If they deny the world the powerful generosity of God and replace it with a narrow self-protectionist arrogance, God will declare that its time has run out.

Why, then, does Jesus suddenly encourage his friends to pray and to forgive? Doesn't this seem rather odd, given what he has just done to the people who were 'innocently' going about their normal business before he disrupted their routines? Well, perhaps the answer is more challenging than we might like to think. Anger and passion for God, his will and his ways are not to be rooted in narrow vindictiveness or blind self-righteousness. Passion for God can only be genuinely exercised in a godly way when born out of godly compassion for those who cannot recognise their own blindness. If we cannot forgive and love, then we should not begin to express anger and pretend that we are being faithful to God's call. At the heart of God's passion lies mercy and forgiveness; if his people's behaviour suggests a different priority, then they have missed the point.

The link between God and his people is made absolutely explicit when Jesus, as in the Lord's Prayer, makes God's forgiveness of us dependent on our forgiveness of those who have offended us. Forgiveness – as Bonhoeffer protested in relation to grace – is never cheap and always demanding. But, if God's people are to bear his name and claim his character, then they have to offer a representation of that character in the way they order their lives and priorities.

Israel's national life and Temple practices did not look anything like a reflection of the passion of a merciful, generous God for all the people of his world. Jesus saw this clearly and pronounced a sad judgement. And then he fulfilled in himself exactly that which the Temple was supposed to represent. And, if the writing was on the wall for the Jerusalem Temple, so was the death warrant now signed for the living Temple, Jesus the messiah.

Lord God, help your people to reflect you, your generous love and passionate character. Preserve us from arrogance and the easy association of our narrow self-interests with your broad and limitless vision for the whole of your world. Amen.

TUESDAY (HOLY WEEK)

MARK 13:1–37 WARNING SIGNS

IT is one of life's more unnerving experiences to sit on a bus or a train and have the person next to you begin to warn you in hushed tones about the imminent end of the world. It presents you with one of life's more troublesome dilemmas: sit and listen ... or make your excuses and leave pronto. Sometimes these 'prophets' are crazy, but sometimes they are just people with an odd way of reading the Bible, an over-fertile imagination and/or a propensity to credulity.

Passages such as Mark 13 have all-too-frequently been taken as speaking of the end of the world, the ultimate judgement of God and the consigning of humanity to heaven or hell. But a simple reading of the text makes it clear that such a reading is absurd. As we have noted throughout this book, Jesus is trying to open the eyes and minds of his friends to understand the nature of God's true kingdom and their place within it. He is trying to prepare the ground for when the penny will finally drop and the pieces will fall into place; then they will make sense of him, his teaching, his healings and his death. Until this process runs its course (and Jesus knows that it cannot be rushed), all he can do is say the things that might make sense only much later on in their experience.

The other point to recognise here is that the disciples yet again don't grasp Jesus' warnings. Jesus has been in and around the Temple ever since his return to the city from Jericho. He has cleared the place out, taught the people and been challenged by the religious teachers and lawyers, and he has meditated on the significance and fate of the place. The Temple is the locus of God's promised presence and the token of his vindication. It is a magnificent building, dominating the city and its environs, a symbol of permanence and solidity. It is huge, and it shows no evidence of imminent collapse.

So, when Jesus responds to the wondrous admiration of the disciples as they look at the Temple, it is no wonder that they are a little bemused. Jesus tells them that this great building, these huge stones, will soon be torn apart, destroyed by those whose intention it will be to humiliate and destroy the people once and for all. But Jesus is not simply predicting the end of things as these people know them; rather, he is trying to impress upon them the fact that this traumatic ending will also be the painful beginning of something new – a new age. He likens this to the experience of a woman in childbirth enduring the uncontrollable pains of labour before experiencing the joy of the new life that has been born. Just as the language of creation in Genesis evokes a picture of God giving birth to the created order, so does Jesus use the same image to give a right perspective to what is going to happen to the disciples after Jesus has departed from them.

The Book of Revelation does a similar job. Written not as a timetable for the end, but as a vivid and coded message of encouragement to those who are in the midst of terrible persecution and suffering on account of their faith, Revelation uses apocalyptic language to exhort, encourage, comfort and warn. The pain and suffering might be acute and there might appear to be no end, but hang on in there – you will be vindicated, and even death will not have the last word. As a rabbi once said of the struggles in Israel between Jews and Palestinians: 'Sometimes it seems that there is no light at the end of the tunnel. But it is not because the light is not there, it is because the tunnel is not straight!' In the midst of persecution and loss and confusion, you will be tempted to give up, to wonder whether the whole thing has been a con; but hang on in to the end and you will see that it is God who has the final word.

This reinforces what Jesus has been trying to say to those who are soon to watch him suffer and die. They will find their grasp of his message confused by these unwelcome and incomprehensible events: the messiah is supposed to triumph over the Roman oppressors, not be executed by them. So, is he just another conman, or are we missing something here? Well, Jesus recognises that the real Temple (himself) is to be destroyed shortly, but the actual Temple building will also eventually be torn down. Both events will cry out for a 'repentance' on the part of the people – an openness to thinking in a new way about God, the world and people. The convulsions that will torment their world will place Jesus' friends in a painful place where God's purposes and the world's agonies meet: they must be prepared and they must learn to be patient when the time comes, always seeing the present experience in the light of the bigger picture of God's promises and activity.

The destruction of Jerusalem came about in AD 70 after a four-year war. Josephus writes in vivid and gory detail about the terrible suffering that people endured while besieged by the Roman armies. The Temple was desecrated by the introduction of pagan 'idols', thus representing the replacement of God with the arrogance of triumphalist human powermongers. The Temple was eventually destroyed, thereby marking the 'end of the world' for many people. The language Jesus uses reflects the apocalyptic language of the Old Testament prophets; banal language will not do justice to the enormity and horror of these (literally) world-shattering events.

All of this will vindicate Jesus' words and actions. The Temple has, by its appeal to narrow nationalism, failed in its calling to be a light to the world, demonstrating God's character and grace to all people; and now it is being discarded. The real locus of God's presence and kingdom turns out to have been this man who came proclaiming good news and calling people to look, see, think, believe and live differently. And, just as the tenants in the parable of chapter 12 are preoccupied with their present well-being, Jesus warns against introspection by his followers and friends. They are to stay awake, keep alert, watching and interpreting the signs of the times – always watching for the signs of God's activity in the world and waiting for his promise to be fulfilled.

These warnings were all about the destruction of Jerusalem and the Temple in AD 70, but the warning to Jesus' followers remains the same: the ending of a 'world' is always also the birth pangs of a new 'world'. Death does not have the final word; God will bring new life out of the ashes of the old. So, don't be afraid; watch and listen; and don't give up.

Lord God, thank you for the patience of your people throughout the ages who have remained faithful to you and your call. Help us to learn from Jesus' warnings and to remain faithful to you – whatever the evidence of the world around us might suggest. Amen.

WEDNESDAY (HOLY WEEK)

MARK 14:1–11   ANOINTED AT BETHANY

MARK'S narrative is driving towards a climax. Jesus has entered the city, and the plots are thickening behind his back. The Passover fervour is building, and the authorities know that time is now short if they are to rid themselves of this troublesome preacher. But, while they plot and scheme and try to find ways of doing their dirty deed that will leave them unsullied (either morally or in the eyes of the people who might otherwise rise up against them), Jesus goes to Bethany with his friends and shares the hospitality of Simon the leper.

Again, the contrasts are prominent: the men blindly plot while an anonymous woman does the right thing; she uses her wealth while the men condemn her for wasting it on Jesus when it could have been used to relieve the lot of the poor – although the implication here is that they didn't necessarily use the resources they themselves had for the same purpose. This woman might not have known the full import of what she was doing, but Jesus felt the painful, poignant, fearful significance of her action: he was being anointed with oil in preparation for his death. The men plan his destruction while the woman affirms his dignity. The men work out how to break his body while the woman spontaneously does something beautiful, precious and honouring to his body.

This beautifully illustrates a question that runs through the gospel like the wording through a stick of seaside rock: why do some people respond well to Jesus and his good news and others respond badly? Or, to focus it more acutely: for whom is Jesus good news and for whom is he bad news? It would appear that he was good news for people who had no illusions about themselves and who had got used to being told bad news about themselves. People warmed to Jesus when they heard that they mattered to God and that even they were included in the community of God's people. Those who thought of Jesus and his proclamation as bad news were those who were either unable or unwilling to 'see' differently, to be open to the possibility that their religious world-view might just be in need of a little reshaping, to have their authority or position questioned or their status amended. And, by and large, these were the religious people who spent their time trying to 'get it right' with God, studying the Scriptures and longing for God's coming liberation and vindication.

This must surely contain a warning to those who think of themselves as 'biblical' or 'close' to God: we are in most danger of missing the point, of confusing means with ends, or of shaping God and his messiah in an image that conforms to our preferences.

Anyway, by describing the Bethany event in the way he does – enveloping the anointing within the plotting of the authorities and the treachery of Judas – Mark seems to be inviting the reader or hearer to place him- or herself within the scene. As Jesus prepares for his death, surrounded by people who still don't know what is about to happen around them and to them, whose side would I be on? Would I be pouring scorn on those who demonstrate their love of Jesus in ways I might find embarrassing, or would I be pouring ointment on his head as an act of expensive, extravagant love? Would I calculate the monetary value of the goods used in this act of generous devotion, or would I have 'repented' and now be seeing through new eyes, eyes that see God, the world, people and 'things' differently? These are not easy questions to answer.

Whereas in the previous chapter the focus is essentially on the eventual destruction of the Temple, the focus in this passage is clearly on the destruction of the Temple that is Jesus. The disciples still seem oblivious to the imminence of the horrors and world-shattering events about to break upon them in Jerusalem. They expect to be celebrating the Passover in a couple of days' time, but this time eagerly expecting the imminence of God's new reign to be enacted through his messiah. Despite all that Jesus has told them and shown them, they still don't fully understand what is to happen. And this act of extravagant 'waste' is lost on them. The dramatic power of this burial rite somehow passes them by – as has much else in the last couple of years while they accompanied Jesus on his remarkable journey through the lives and politics of his people.

It is possible to ignore an element of this encounter which also speaks powerfully to people who express love and devotion in words but fail to back them up in action. This woman appears to say nothing. She doesn't attempt to justify her action and doesn't see any need to explain it. She simply breaks open the jar of ointment and lets it speak for itself as it runs down the head of the soon-to-be-executed Jesus. Others may wish to use words to praise or condemn her or analyse the motivation behind this surprising action, but she need say nothing: the action can speak for itself.

In a world in which language is cheap and words cascade on and around us without respite, there is something quietly powerful about a woman who sees no need to justify herself. Others may criticise or praise her, but Jesus is the only defender she needs.

And all this still leaves the reader with the unanswered question: where would I place myself in the matrix of people and perspectives represented in this encounter? Furthermore, what does my answer say about me, my openness to 'repentance', my understanding of Jesus and who he is for?

Lord God, you call us, like the woman who anointed Jesus at Bethany, to love you without calculation. So, move in our hearts and minds that we too might express our love for and devotion to you without the need to justify or explain it. Grant us the grace to accept the offerings of others, even if we question their value or appropriateness. Amen.

MAUNDY THURSDAY (HOLY WEEK)

MARK 14:12–25   THE LAST SUPPER

WORDS are sometimes not enough. A ship is launched not by the utterance of mere words but by the smashing of a bottle against its hull before it moves down the slipway into the water for the first time. A marriage is solemnised by words, but it is the giving and receiving of a ring that makes it visible. Love of Jesus can be expressed in words, but the pouring of expensive ointment speaks a language that makes words seem inadequate. And Jesus leaves his friends not with mere words but with an action, a familiar action that takes an everyday ritual (sharing food), applies it to a particular common memory (Passover), then resignifies it in a way that makes the ordinary extraordinary and roots it at the heart of the future common life of his friends (communion).

The Passover meal is no ordinary meal. It is not akin to a birthday party or a dinner party. It is perhaps what Christmas dinner ought to be – a powerful celebration of God's irruption into the world in this baby who will one day swap the wood of the manger for the wood of the gallows, but who will en route turn the world upside down. The Passover meal was pregnant with significance for the Jews, powerfully moving, shocking and encouraging.

The exodus from hundreds of years of exile and oppression at the hands of the Egyptian overlords came not as the result of human ingenuity or military power but by the initiative and grace of God. The earliest credal statement in the Hebrew Bible (Deuteronomy 26:5–11) uses verbs to emphasise that the liberation of God's people was God's activity, not theirs. The Passover narrative reinforces this, making it clear that there is no place for human pride here; we are here not because of our own skill and strength, but because God has done this for us. The people of God are never to forget their story or their theology, and this remembering must cause them to reflect God's liberating grace and generosity in how they live with and treat others – especially vulnerable people such as defenceless foreigners and poor people.

The Passover was not only an opportunity each year to look back and remember the foundational story of the people; it also served to make a powerful statement of theology: God is sovereign and his people are free ... despite the evidence of the world around us. God's people might be oppressed and it might appear that Caesar is Lord of all the world; but we know that empires come and go, that God will neither be mocked nor rushed, and that although we appear to be enslaved our spirits are free to see and live differently. The Passover celebration looks back to the exodus but compels us to live counter-culturally in the present while looking forward to our future liberation. Hence, God's people are set free to live in a way that refuses to accept the apparent 'real' world as the 'true' world.

When Jesus and his friends share this supper in the city, the atmosphere is surely tense. All the messianic hopes are in ferment with confusion about Jesus' role in the coming liberation. Religion and politics are intertwined in an act (the meal) that is at the same time both celebratory and seditious. Then Jesus takes the familiar elements of bread and wine, symbols of Israel's history and identity, and resignifies them in the clearest way possible. The exodus was God's initiative, cost blood and set a messy and ungrateful people free – free not to enjoy 'being free' but to fulfil their calling to be God's people for the sake of the world, to be a light to the world. And what Jesus has tried to explain cryptically throughout his journey with his friends he now makes explicit. 'I am Israel,' he says, 'fulfilling the calling that has always been Israel's, and this is to be exercised in a new exodus that will be achieved for you (not by you) and will cost blood. I will be broken for you in order that you might be broken for the world for which you are called in my name.' Thus Jesus finally makes the connections in a way that one day soon will make sense to these soon-to-be-broken disciples.

Yet there is something in the context of this story that needs to speak powerfully to those who even today claim to be followers of this same Jesus. Jesus invited to this supper a ragbag of people whose theology was in need of reshaping, whose grasp of Jesus' identity was fragile, and whose ability to get on with each other was questionable. And that is the point: Jesus invites to his supper – this uniquely life- and world-changing supper – those who will yet go on to betray him, deny knowing him, desert him and doubt him. All that matters is that it is Jesus who does the inviting.

So, what does this say to a Christian community in which some are excluded from sharing in this meal on grounds of non-conformity to a particular theological detail or ethical prescription? By what authority does one church decide to dis-invite another from communion? By what spirit does one part of one church decide to break communion with another as a means of asserting its own particular 'orthodoxy' or political power? If Jesus is the one who invites even fickle followers like me, who am I to say who else should or should not be invited to the supper? This is Jesus' meal in which he makes clear that his followers are – whether they like it or not – one body, his body. It is nothing short of shameful that Christians so easily arrogate to themselves the right to exclude from communion those who don't 'fit', even if such people find themselves in the company of that ragbag of people invited by Jesus himself.

This supper, pregnant with emotion and power for all sorts of reasons, compels Jesus' followers to look back and remember their story (their need of God's liberating generosity); to look around (at a broken world in need of a united church that lives according to a counter-cultural mandate); to look forward (to the kingdom that Jesus has inaugurated and that God will complete in Jesus, causing us to live as if that new age were already here); and to look in (examining ourselves in humility to see if we are reflecting the self-giving life of Jesus himself whose body we are called to be).

Lord God, in bread and wine we remember who we are, whence we have come and where our future lies. Empower your people throughout the world to live in this world but not being of it; to love it but not be enslaved to its dominant 'reality'. May your Church be a proclaimer of the good news of reconciliation, not a reminder of the bad news of the world's fragmentation. Amen.

GOOD FRIDAY (HOLY WEEK)

MARK 14:26–15:39   ARRESTED AND KILLED

THIS great and tragic drama is reaching its climax. If the thunder clouds were rolling in earlier, they are now making their noises heard, and the sky is getting darker and more menacing. The pace seems to take on an extra urgency as the reader begins to see what is happening … while the disciples don't quite get it. This part of the gospel narrative needs to be read in one large chunk. To split it up into little bits detracts from the dynamic of the text and diminishes the impact of the events as they unfurl.

However, having read the story through, it is possible to look at the different characters in it and ask questions of them in turn.

Jesus has eaten his final meal with his friends and has resignified the common elements of bread and wine to represent his body and blood. He predicts (again) the failure of the disciples firstly to stay the course and secondly to fulfil the promise of their own bravado. In the Garden of Gethsemane, Jesus faces not just a notional choice but a real and very powerful crisis. It is clear from his agony in the Garden that the temptations he faced in the desert at the commencement of his public ministry have not gone away. He longs for a way out, but his prayer leads him to hold to God's will and God's way, not shunning the hard road in favour of an easy escape.

When Judas greets Jesus with a kiss, Jesus surrenders and makes clear the fact that he is not a military messiah come to liberate the people from the Roman oppressors. Indeed, this might have been Judas' attempt to force Jesus' hand in declaring his messianic identity. But Jesus has spent the whole of his three-year journey through this gospel undermining the received assumption about who the messiah might be and what the messiah would do. Weapons of violence have no place in the kingdom of this messiah.

Facing charges by the authorities, Jesus keeps silent. Their charges are their affair. But, when asked to declare his identity, he finally exposes what he has for so long wanted kept secret: that he is indeed the messiah of God. Earlier, Jesus asked Peter and his friends to say with their own mouths who they thought Jesus is; now he speaks for himself too. And it is this claim that directly leads to the charge of blasphemy and the sentence of death. The horrible irony about to be played out is that the people are going to deride and torture as a mock 'King of the Jews' the actual King of the Jews. The authorities have got their man and have finally found a way of getting him out of their hair; so, they manipulate the Roman overlords and whip up the people for a spectacle of death. And, in the midst of this horror, Jesus takes the place of Barabbas, the innocent replacing the guilty on the gallows.

A reading of this long section of Mark's text makes it clear that Jesus got nailed because of his messianic pretensions. All that he has said and hinted at throughout the journey has led to this point where Jesus publicly claims his throne and appears to be humiliated by being 'enthroned' on a cross

– apparently a victim of the powers of Rome, who once again have demonstrated their invincibility and their cruel dominance in the things of this world. Jesus, the 'King', is shown to be no king; the powerful has been shockingly shown to be powerless; the one so close to God has been heard to claim that he has been abandoned by his God. The stone Temple still stands proudly in the city while this 'temple' is dismantled outside the city where the rubbish is dumped. What a shambles. What an embarrassment.

The *disciples* are confused. They are aware of the growing threat, but do not seem to grasp the possibility that Jesus might be violently wrested from them. They repeatedly protest their allegiance, possibly on the assumption that any self-sacrifice will prove unnecessary once Jesus asserts his messianic authority and takes his rightful place of power and governance. But, yet again, we see the disciples portrayed as people like you and me: unrealistic about their own commitment and endurance, fickle in their affections, lacking in courage when tempted with an easier option, running away in shame when the 'world' appears to be falling apart.

These people are real. They are not figures of propaganda, beefed up to improve their reputations. They have consistently been portrayed as people who fail to grasp Jesus' mission, regularly misunderstand his teaching, never come to terms with his theology and always overestimate their own commitment to him. These are people who harbour great illusions about themselves and their characters, people who (to quote Paul from Romans 12) think more highly of themselves than they ought. So, their illusions are going to be dispelled and their self-image shattered by the events now unravelling.

The *Jewish authorities* have finally found a way to rid themselves of this embarrassing and challenging threat ... and it hasn't cost them much either. The *Romans* have averted a riot and kept the colonised native elite reasonably content. The *people* have had a bit of excitement – something to help them exorcise the energy and anger generated by the hopes of Passover being mocked by the reality of occupation and captivity. The story has reached its climax, and the itinerant preacher from up north has finally been removed from the scene. So, we can assume that everyone is now happy and relieved that an unhappy and embarrassing episode in the nation's life has finally come to an end.

But Mark is not finished ... and, more importantly, neither is God.

The world will soon catch a glimpse of the revolutionary truth that the King of the Jews is seen to be such precisely by his remaining on the cross and dying there – not by saving his own skin with a dramatic act of self-preservation. Religious mockery that invokes the old prophets (Elijah) will soon be revealed to have been misplaced – for this messiah is actually fulfilling in his own life and death what Elijah and the prophets were trying to tell Israel was their calling by God from the beginning.

All these ironies are beginning to become clear to Mark's reader. And then, with dramatic impact, the curtain of the Temple is ripped in two, thus opening the way for people to have direct access to the holy place where God is – and it is a pagan Gentile who recognises who Jesus really is. As with the contrast in Mark 10 between those close to Jesus (James and John) and the useless beggar (Bartimaeus), it is the 'blind' who see and the 'seeing' who prove to be blind. In the death of Jesus, the world is turned upside down: those who protect God as 'their' vindicator fail to recognise that the 'unclean' will now see more clearly who he is and respond to his call.

This is world-shattering stuff. And it is a stark, deafening reminder to the people who see themselves as God's that it is only by sharing in the mission of Jesus to the whole world – including the 'world' on our own doorstep – in his way and in his name that we may dare to call ourselves Christian.

Lord God, may we die with Jesus to all the pretensions and arrogances of this world and put to death the petty religious power games we play as the Church. Thank you for taking with you – and not despising – disciples who are as messy today as they were on Good Friday in Jerusalem. Amen.

SATURDAY (HOLY WEEK)

MARK 15:40–7 DEAD AND BURIED

JESUS died and was dead. Completely dead. When he was buried in the tomb, he was not simply recovering from a bit of a swoon. At the risk of hitting this nail too hard on the head, let me say it again: Jesus was dead, as dead as dead can be.

If you are wondering why that needs to be said so clearly and repeatedly, it is because many Christians seem either not to really believe it or not to understand it. There are examples of contemporary worship songs that betray a rather over-spiritualised theology by suggesting that Jesus came back to life. But that speaks of resuscitation where the gospels speak of resurrection – as Paul put it, 'God raised Christ from the dead'. Well, more of this anon; but suffice it here simply to note that Jesus died, and his body was removed from the cross and placed in a tomb.

However, Mark still has surprises for us. There is no opportunity yet to relax and catch our breath. We noted earlier in the gospel how Mark contrasts the courage and devotion of the women in Jesus' life with the rather fickle and self-deluded bravado of the men. It is the woman with the precious ointment who gets it right for Jesus while the men stand round missing the point. And here again, in this simple account of the burial of Jesus, it is the women who have stayed at the scene of horror and watched Jesus die. It is the women who attend the body of Christ. It is women – in the context of a patriarchal society and religion – who honour the body of Christ when the men who have pleaded loyalty appear to be missing.

Maybe it is possible to read too much into this from a perspective gleaned 2,000 years later in a western secular culture. But maybe there is something here that should profoundly disturb the reader. It is the people of little value (women) who get it right for Jesus. They are not recorded as protesting undying love for Jesus; but they demonstrate it nonetheless. Yet, those who use fine words and make their brave protestations appear to be absent when their words need to be cashed in. The truth is always to be gauged not from what we claim with words but with what we reveal in actions.

However, the women are not alone. We know little about Joseph of Arimathea except that he was one of those present during the deliberations about Jesus' fate. We read that he was 'himself waiting for the kingdom of God'. We do not know whether or not he argued Jesus' case before the Sanhedrin or if he exposed his own suspicions about Jesus' true identity. We do know, though, that he took the risk of asking Pilate for the body and tended to it at his own expense prior to interring the corpse in a tomb and sealing the entrance.

In doing all this, Joseph was making himself 'unclean'. He would be touching the dead body of Jesus and thus making himself contaminated, unable to join in the rituals prescribed for the Sabbath day. The cost of tending the body of Christ is not insignificant for this man, who risks much by his brave generosity.

Nevertheless, the real significance of this part of Mark's story can be said to lie in a full stop. The corpse is laid in the tomb, the tomb is sealed, the women note its location ... and then there is a gap from the beginning of the Sabbath until the morning after the ending of the Sabbath. Nothing happens, and nothing is recorded. The Sabbath passes, and Mark tells us nothing about what happened or where the disciples were or what the mood among the people in Jerusalem was. We can imagine the satisfaction felt by the authorities and the relief felt by the Romans. We can also look from a distance and observe the horrible irony of the Sabbath being celebrated by a people who have just rid themselves of the Lord of the Sabbath. And we have no option but to imagine the state of the friends of Jesus.

We must remember that the disciples started out on a journey with Jesus two or three years before. They have heard him proclaim the 'Good News' that the kingdom of God is now among them, and they have found themselves gradually having the 'lens behind their eyes' reshaped so that they might see and think about God, the world and people differently. This is what we have understood 'repentance' to be from the beginning of Jesus' ministry. They have seen miracles and joined in the exercise of Jesus' mission to bring healing and reconciliation. They have listened to his teaching about God and his people and have tried to absorb it despite their limited vision and fragile grasp of his meaning or its implications. They have accompanied their friend to the heart of darkness and promised to stand until the end with Jesus. They still expected him to lead the people into the new age of freedom and peace, but they have now just witnessed his execution amid rank mockery and venomous humiliation.

For these distraught and probably disillusioned people, the Sabbath must have seemed empty, frightening and endless. Bereavement is a terrible experience anyway; but the really hard bit is when you wake up after the first night of attempted sleep, and the horrible, unavoidable reality of loss cannot be disguised. The friends of Jesus had to spend a day of emptiness and shock, reshaping their mindset yet again, fearing for their lives and wondering what might happen next. Their world has fallen apart, and there is no Jesus figure to help them put it back together again. They are surely desolate and distressed.

But this day, with all its horror, emptiness, confusion and contradictions, has to be lived through if discipleship is to be real. Easter Day will not be rushed, and the shock of Good Friday will not be quickly turned into delight. God's people – the friends of Jesus – have to stick with the emptiness and live through it; they must resist the temptation to run away from it or to ignore it in favour of the joy that will follow. For these friends of Jesus did not know what was to follow – despite having been taught by Jesus about a resurrection that they could not fit into this current scenario.

Followers of Jesus must learn to stay on Saturday and live with the unresolved emptiness of it. It is as much part of the Christian journey as is Easter Day. And it must not be avoided or cheapened. Where people find themselves in this dark and empty place, they are to be honoured and accompanied – not whisked out to the easy place.

Jesus is dead … and the world has turned very dark. Imagine it.

Lord God, you did not spare the disciples this dark day and this nightmare experience. Forgive us when we recognise your presence only in the good experiences of life and worship. Help us to resist the temptation to run away when we are empty and confused, enabled by your grace to live through the dark time, risking everything to be surprised by you. Amen.

EASTER DAY

MARK 16   CHRIST IS RISEN

WOMEN have come out of this gospel very well. They get on and 'do' while the men are somewhere else 'being'. The women who watched Jesus die on the cross also followed Joseph of Arimathea and noted the location of the tomb. They have sat out the Sabbath day and after sunset have bought spices for the tending of the decomposing body of Jesus. At first light, they proceed to the tomb and are preoccupied with the very practical matter of how to gain access to the tomb by removing the stone from its entrance. This detail is important. The women intend to visit a corpse and do not expect to find anything other than a logistical problem with a gravestone. They do not expect to find an absent body or an empty tomb. And, when they find the tomb occupied only by a man in white who tells them that Jesus is on his way to Galilee, they do not burst into a joyful celebration of the resurrection; in fact, they are shocked and distressed and flee away in fear.

So, what is going on here? The first thing to ask is what this says about the women. As with the disciples throughout this gospel, the women are real and recognisable as real people, not figments of a propagandist's imagination. They still don't get it. But it rams home the point that it is not the fact of *resurrection* that transforms lives; rather, it is an eventual encounter with the one who has been resurrected.

The second thing to note is that (as has been recognised by many scholars and commentators) the ending of the gospel seems to be missing. The two alternative endings somehow don't quite fit, but it is unlikely that the gospel ended with the women's fear. The great thing about missing the ending, however, is that it leaves us hanging in mid-air, needing to read the whole narrative again, questioning the way Mark has told the story, and asking ourselves to what climax he was driving us.

Jesus has been finally crucified because he has claimed to be fulfilling in himself the calling that was always Israel's – to be the servant people of God who were called for the sake of the world. The Temple and all the religious provisions of the system were designed not as ends in themselves but as means to remind the people of their calling, its cost and its purpose. The failure of the people and the Temple was compounded by the messianic hopes they harboured and the deliverance from Roman oppression that they longed for. These events would vindicate them before the world and usher in the new age of God's reign. But Jesus took these longings and understandings and turned them on their head. The messianic calling would not involve the eviction of the Romans, and the calling of the people would not be fulfilled in the ways they had assumed. Jesus challenged the religious status quo and found the leaders unwilling to countenance any change in their thinking or theological framework. They would not 'repent' and see through a lens shaped like Jesus' notion of the kingdom of God.

The disciples were a group of ordinary people who did not choose each other but were invited by

Jesus to set out on a journey with him in ignorance of what might happen along the way or where it might end. This journey involved them in re-envisaging God and the world and learning what it might mean to be God's renewed people. They were hopeless at this task, and yet Jesus did not ever reject them for their fragile humanity. He stayed faithful to them to the end and beyond, even though they betrayed him, deserted him, denied him, doubted him and failed to understand him.

But the real power of this remarkable journey lies in the contradiction Jesus offers to the norms of this world. What looks to be weak, defeated and mocked turns out to be vindicated, renewed and victorious. In a world in which power is wielded by people with large weapons and loud threats, Jesus stands naked and challenges the powermongers to do their worst. And on this Easter morning, in an empty tomb occupied by a man in white and several frightened women, the world discovers that death, violence and destruction do not have the final word. The relentless cycle of violence and revenge has to be broken, and that is what Jesus has done. He has taken all that the world in its stubborn blindness and fear can throw at him, and he has absorbed its power, refusing to hurl it back. By dying, he has allowed death its power ... and then stripped it of its power and threat by being raised by God.

Christians are not to trust in resurrection. They are to trust in the God who raised Jesus and promises to do the same for those who are 'in Christ'. Christian faith cannot – despite some of the dubious theology in some of our songs – rest in a Christ who 'came back to life'. Christian faith must be firmly rooted in God himself – the God who created, sustains, renews, loves and dies for the world. It is God who raises from the dead who also calls his people (as he has done from the very beginning) to lay down their lives for the sake of the world. The Church, that ragbag of saints and sinners who all-too-often look very like the disciples of Mark's gospel, is called to be a people who deny the powermongers the fear on which their threats rely. They are to be a people who recognise the power of death and destruction but refuse to let them have the final word. They are people who are not afraid to confront the world's injustices at great cost to themselves. And they are people who know how to look beyond the immediate evidence of decay to see the confusing, bewildering hint of resurrection and new life.

Mark brings us to Easter Day less with joy than with a profound challenge. Are we prepared even now to have our mindset transformed by seeing through the eyes of Jesus and 'being' his body on earth? Are we willing to trust ourselves completely to what we see when we look through his eyes at God, the world and ourselves? Are we able and willing to see the shape of the kingdom of God as Jesus saw it, taught it, enacted it and proclaimed it?

Only if we can affirm all this will we be able to be the body of Christ, inviting people of today to 'repent', 'believe the good news' ... that the kingdom of God is indeed near. As the risen body of Jesus bore the wound marks in his hands and feet and side, so will his Church be exposed to the realities of the world, often ridiculed by a world that works to a different agenda, but empowered by his spirit to be fearless in offering a different way of seeing ... and thinking ... and living ... and dying.

PERSONAL REFLECTION

Where would I place myself in the story from Palm Sunday to Easter Day? With which characters do I most identify myself?

Am I one who 'breaks the body' or 'anoints the body' of Christ?

GROUP DISCUSSION

1. How would we recognise a 'prophet' today?

2. Why do we find it so easy to limit the scope of God's generosity and grace, thereby excluding people Jesus might have called to follow him in our company? Why did Jesus share his last supper with such a messy group of failures ... and what does this say to us about the nature and welcome of the Church?

3. What does it mean for us to 'live through the emptiness of Saturday'?

4. What light does God's raising of Jesus from the dead shine on our view of the world's violence, threat, fear and destructiveness?

5. What sort of discipleship might the Jesus of Mark's gospel be calling us to undertake?

OTHER BOOKS BY NICK BAINES

Speedbumps and Potholes

Looking for signs of God in the Everyday

(ISBN 0 7152 0806 3)

Entertaining, often amusing and always thought-provoking, these 42 short reflections are not meant to offer the final word on the meaning of God, life, the universe and everything. Instead, they come from observation and ordinary, everyday experience. They offer the reader glimpses of a new perspective in daily life.

> 'On a blustery cold day, as I write this, Nick Baines has worked his ecclesiastical magic and made me feel much sunnier. And that's a God-given gift.'
>
> Sarah Kennedy, BBC Radio 2 presenter

> 'Thought-provoking with zest, careful reflection and great fun ... This is spirituality for busy people who enjoy the richness of God's creation.'
>
> The Revd Dr Richard A. Burridge,
> Dean of King's College, London

Jesus and People Like Us

The Transforming Power of grace

(ISBN 0 7152 0820 9)

'... a book from which I could learn, grow and feel empowered. This is a book about real people with a true story that can help us today. I got so much out of this book.'

Daleep Mukarji, Director, Christian Aid

'Baines clearly has an affection for and an immersion in scripture. With insight and integrity, he shares a panoramic vision of the ministry of Jesus. His agility of mind, clarity of writing and refreshing insights make the book as much a companion to the gospels as a commentary on them.'

John Bell, Iona Community

Nick Baines takes us on the journey from Galilee to Jerusalem taken by Jesus and his followers. As we accompany them, we can listen in and reflect on what was happening:

'The people chosen by Jesus to follow him on his journey were invited to leave their familiar surroundings for an unknown future. They were introduced to people and situations that made them uncomfortable. Their religious suppositions were challenged to their roots. Their world view would be threatened, disturbed and reshaped. They discovered resources within themselves they never knew they had. They were invigorated, enthused, emboldened and excited, as well as horrified, frightened, disillusioned and humiliated.'

The book aims to encourage those who sometimes wonder where God is and who wonder why he seems to have gone missing. For all who aspire to live the Christian life, this book is both liberating and encouraging.

AVAILABLE FROM YOUR LOCAL CHRISTIAN BOOKSHOP
OR CONTACT 0870 787 1211
FOR HELP IN OBTAINING YOUR COPY.